C000157829

A RECORD OF
MY VINYL

All rights reserved.
Published in the United States by Clarkson Potter/Publishers,
an imprint of the Crown Publishing Group, a division of
Penguin Random House LLC, New York.
www.crownpublishing.com
www.clarksonpotter.com

CLARKSON POTTER is a trademark and POTTER with colophon
is a registered trademark of Penguin Random House LLC.

Grateful acknowledgment is made to the following:

Goldmine © Grading Guide courtesy of Krause Publications,
a division of F+W Media, Inc.

NPR and Jack White for permission to reprint a quote from Jack
White, in "Jack White's Record Label: Old Sounds, New Tricks,"
recorded on *All Things Considered,* April 10, 2010. All rights
reserved. Reprinted by permission of NPR and Jack White.

Excerpt on page 6 from DUST & GROOVES: ADVENTURES IN
RECORD COLLECTING by Eilon Paz, copyright © 2014 by Dust
& Grooves LLC. Used by permission of Ten Speed Press, an
imprint of the Crown Publishing Group, a division of Penguin
Random House LLC. All rights reserved.

Library of Congress Cataloging-in-Publication Data
Names: Potter Style.
Title: A record of my vinyl: a collector's catalog/Potter Style.
Description: First edition / New York: Clarkson Potter/Publishers,
[2017]
Identifiers: LCCN 2016031114/ISBN 9780804189606 (non-
traditional : alk. paper)
Subjects: LCSH: Sound recordings—Collectors and collecting—
Forms. /Blank-books.
Classification: LCC ML111.5.S83 2017 /DDC 780.26—dc23
LC record available at https://lccn.loc.gov/2016031114

ISBN 978-0-8041-8960-6

Printed in China

Cover and interior design by Stephanie Huntwork
Written by Brian Borsics
Cover photograph: (record) donatas1205/Shutterstock

10 9 8 7 6 5 4 3 2 1

First Edition

A RECORD OF

MY VINYL

A COLLECTOR'S CATALOG

POTTER

Vinyl records are back. Well, technically, they never left, but since the early 2000s, vinyl sales around the world have surged as a new generation of audiophiles joins the ranks of those who remained loyal to the format. Once we turned our attention to digital technology, then magnetic tape, vinyl, and other things analog were largely replaced, first by CDs and then by MP3s, until eventually music—a seemingly limitless supply of everything from Bieber to Beethoven—came streaming at us from every Internet port on earth.

It is not that our reliance on digital has faded (its obvious importance need not be stated here), but now that the honeymoon phase is over, audiophiles and casual listeners everywhere are either sticking to or flocking back to vinyl.

WHY VINYL IS SO COOL

Vinyl recordings are tangible and tactile—things we can cherish, share, and showcase; they also require a level of care not needed by cassette tapes or CDs. Furthermore, the love we feel for the music that moves us could never be adequately conveyed by pointing to our music-streaming subscription or the pile of CDs that live on the floorboard of our cars. Aside from poetry and prose, only a meticulously doted-upon collection of vinyl recordings could convey that passion. And to cultivate a collection so aptly demonstrative of our character and passions, we must take the time to seek out the discs we add to it, exercise the patience necessary to protect and maintain it, and share our living space with it, constantly organizing the artifacts that have earned their place.

Did you know, when deciding which format we would launch into space toward some unknown intelligence—for the job of sonically representing humanity and earth to anyone who may be listening—we sent golden records? Fastened to the hull of Voyager spacecrafts 1 and 2, currently hurtling through space at 38,610 miles per hour, are rotatable gold discs; on one side, there are mathematical instructions on how to play them, and on the other is a selection of the sounds of our lives and our world: crashing waves, rolling thunder, and the music of Chuck Berry and Wolfgang Amadeus Mozart. President Jimmy Carter attached the following message:

This is a present from a small, distant world, a token of our sounds, our science, our images, our music, our thoughts and our feelings. We are attempting to survive our time so we may live into yours.

HOW TO USE THIS JOURNAL

You'll find many online resources for cataloging and organizing information about your collection. They're practical and easy. And digital. But if analog is your bag, what is more analog than pen on paper? Use this journal to jot down information and fond memories associated with your discs. Let it stand as the ultimate companion to your collection. State in your Last Will and Testament if this journal should get passed down with your records or buried along with you. At the back, you'll find helpful tips for starting or maintaining a collection—whether your thing is the LP, the 45, or the rare 78 (and information on the difference between the three)—and, finally, wish lists for which albums you care to seek out, so they won't be the ones that got away.

"Until you buy the vinyl record,
  you don't really own the album."
—JACK WHITE

ARTIST	LABEL	
ALBUM	COUNTRY	
CATALOG NO.	YEAR	GRADE

LINER NOTES

ARTIST	LABEL	
ALBUM	COUNTRY	
CATALOG NO.	YEAR	GRADE

LINER NOTES

ARTIST	LABEL	
ALBUM	COUNTRY	
CATALOG NO.	YEAR	GRADE

LINER NOTES

ARTIST	LABEL	
ALBUM	COUNTRY	
CATALOG NO.	YEAR	GRADE

LINER NOTES

ARTIST	LABEL	
ALBUM	COUNTRY	
CATALOG NO.	YEAR	GRADE

LINER NOTES

ARTIST	LABEL	
ALBUM	COUNTRY	
CATALOG NO.	YEAR	GRADE

LINER NOTES

ARTIST	LABEL	
ALBUM	COUNTRY	
CATALOG NO.	YEAR	GRADE

LINER NOTES

ARTIST	LABEL	
ALBUM	COUNTRY	
CATALOG NO.	YEAR	GRADE

LINER NOTES

ARTIST

LABEL

ALBUM

COUNTRY

CATALOG NO.

YEAR

GRADE

LINER NOTES

ARTIST

LABEL

ALBUM

COUNTRY

CATALOG NO.

YEAR

GRADE

LINER NOTES

ARTIST

LABEL

ALBUM

COUNTRY

CATALOG NO.

YEAR

GRADE

LINER NOTES

ARTIST

LABEL

ALBUM

COUNTRY

CATALOG NO.

YEAR

GRADE

LINER NOTES

ARTIST	LABEL	
ALBUM	COUNTRY	
CATALOG NO.	YEAR	GRADE

LINER NOTES

_____

_____

_____

_____

ARTIST	LABEL	
ALBUM	COUNTRY	
CATALOG NO.	YEAR	GRADE

LINER NOTES

_____

_____

_____

_____

ARTIST	LABEL	
ALBUM	COUNTRY	
CATALOG NO.	YEAR	GRADE

LINER NOTES

_____

_____

_____

_____

ARTIST	LABEL	
ALBUM	COUNTRY	
CATALOG NO.	YEAR	GRADE

LINER NOTES

_____

_____

_____

_____

ARTIST	LABEL	
ALBUM	COUNTRY	
CATALOG NO.	YEAR	GRADE

LINER NOTES

_____

_____

_____

_____

_____

ARTIST	LABEL	
ALBUM	COUNTRY	
CATALOG NO.	YEAR	GRADE

LINER NOTES

_____

_____

_____

_____

_____

ARTIST	LABEL	
ALBUM	COUNTRY	
CATALOG NO.	YEAR	GRADE

LINER NOTES

_____

_____

_____

_____

_____

ARTIST	LABEL	
ALBUM	COUNTRY	
CATALOG NO.	YEAR	GRADE

LINER NOTES

_____

_____

_____

_____

ARTIST | LABEL
ALBUM | COUNTRY
CATALOG NO. | YEAR | GRADE
LINER NOTES

ARTIST | LABEL
ALBUM | COUNTRY
CATALOG NO. | YEAR | GRADE
LINER NOTES

ARTIST | LABEL
ALBUM | COUNTRY
CATALOG NO. | YEAR | GRADE
LINER NOTES

ARTIST | LABEL
ALBUM | COUNTRY
CATALOG NO. | YEAR | GRADE
LINER NOTES

ARTIST

ALBUM

CATALOG NO.

LINER NOTES

LABEL

COUNTRY

YEAR

GRADE

ARTIST

ALBUM

CATALOG NO.

LINER NOTES

LABEL

COUNTRY

YEAR

GRADE

ARTIST

ALBUM

CATALOG NO.

LINER NOTES

LABEL

COUNTRY

YEAR

GRADE

ARTIST

ALBUM

CATALOG NO.

LINER NOTES

LABEL

COUNTRY

YEAR

GRADE

CATEGORY

ARTIST	LABEL	
ALBUM	COUNTRY	
CATALOG NO.	YEAR	GRADE

LINER NOTES

ARTIST	LABEL	
ALBUM	COUNTRY	
CATALOG NO.	YEAR	GRADE

LINER NOTES

ARTIST	LABEL	
ALBUM	COUNTRY	
CATALOG NO.	YEAR	GRADE

LINER NOTES

ARTIST	LABEL	
ALBUM	COUNTRY	
CATALOG NO.	YEAR	GRADE

LINER NOTES

ARTIST	LABEL	
ALBUM	COUNTRY	
CATALOG NO.	YEAR	GRADE

LINER NOTES

_____

_____

_____

_____

ARTIST	LABEL	
ALBUM	COUNTRY	
CATALOG NO.	YEAR	GRADE

LINER NOTES

_____

_____

_____

_____

ARTIST	LABEL	
ALBUM	COUNTRY	
CATALOG NO.	YEAR	GRADE

LINER NOTES

_____

_____

_____

_____

ARTIST	LABEL	
ALBUM	COUNTRY	
CATALOG NO.	YEAR	GRADE

LINER NOTES

_____

_____

_____

_____

CATEGORY

ARTIST	LABEL	
ALBUM	COUNTRY	
CATALOG NO.	YEAR	GRADE

LINER NOTES

_____
_____
_____
_____

ARTIST	LABEL	
ALBUM	COUNTRY	
CATALOG NO.	YEAR	GRADE

LINER NOTES

_____
_____
_____
_____

ARTIST	LABEL	
ALBUM	COUNTRY	
CATALOG NO.	YEAR	GRADE

LINER NOTES

_____
_____
_____
_____

ARTIST	LABEL	
ALBUM	COUNTRY	
CATALOG NO.	YEAR	GRADE

LINER NOTES

_____
_____
_____
_____

ARTIST	LABEL	
ALBUM	COUNTRY	
CATALOG NO.	YEAR	GRADE

LINER NOTES

ARTIST	LABEL	
ALBUM	COUNTRY	
CATALOG NO.	YEAR	GRADE

LINER NOTES

ARTIST	LABEL	
ALBUM	COUNTRY	
CATALOG NO.	YEAR	GRADE

LINER NOTES

ARTIST	LABEL	
ALBUM	COUNTRY	
CATALOG NO.	YEAR	GRADE

LINER NOTES

CATEGORY

ARTIST	LABEL	
ALBUM	COUNTRY	
CATALOG NO.	YEAR	GRADE

LINER NOTES

_____

_____

_____

_____

ARTIST	LABEL	
ALBUM	COUNTRY	
CATALOG NO.	YEAR	GRADE

LINER NOTES

_____

_____

_____

ARTIST	LABEL	
ALBUM	COUNTRY	
CATALOG NO.	YEAR	GRADE

LINER NOTES

_____

_____

_____

_____

ARTIST	LABEL	
ALBUM	COUNTRY	
CATALOG NO.	YEAR	GRADE

LINER NOTES

_____

_____

_____

_____

ARTIST

LABEL

ALBUM

COUNTRY

CATALOG NO.

YEAR

GRADE

LINER NOTES

ARTIST

LABEL

ALBUM

COUNTRY

CATALOG NO.

YEAR

GRADE

LINER NOTES

ARTIST

LABEL

ALBUM

COUNTRY

CATALOG NO.

YEAR

GRADE

LINER NOTES

ARTIST

LABEL

ALBUM

COUNTRY

CATALOG NO.

YEAR

GRADE

LINER NOTES

ARTIST	LABEL	
ALBUM	COUNTRY	
CATALOG NO.	YEAR	GRADE

LINER NOTES

ARTIST	LABEL	
ALBUM	COUNTRY	
CATALOG NO.	YEAR	GRADE

LINER NOTES

ARTIST	LABEL	
ALBUM	COUNTRY	
CATALOG NO.	YEAR	GRADE

LINER NOTES

ARTIST	LABEL	
ALBUM	COUNTRY	
CATALOG NO.	YEAR	GRADE

LINER NOTES

ARTIST	LABEL
ALBUM	COUNTRY
CATALOG NO.	YEAR	GRADE

LINER NOTES

ARTIST	LABEL
ALBUM	COUNTRY
CATALOG NO.	YEAR	GRADE

LINER NOTES

ARTIST	LABEL
ALBUM	COUNTRY
CATALOG NO.	YEAR	GRADE

LINER NOTES

ARTIST	LABEL
ALBUM	COUNTRY
CATALOG NO.	YEAR	GRADE

LINER NOTES

CATEGORY

ARTIST

LABEL

ALBUM

COUNTRY

CATALOG NO.

YEAR

GRADE

LINER NOTES

ARTIST

LABEL

ALBUM

COUNTRY

CATALOG NO.

YEAR

GRADE

LINER NOTES

ARTIST

LABEL

ALBUM

COUNTRY

CATALOG NO.

YEAR

GRADE

LINER NOTES

ARTIST

LABEL

ALBUM

COUNTRY

CATALOG NO.

YEAR

GRADE

LINER NOTES

ARTIST

LABEL

ALBUM

COUNTRY

CATALOG NO.

YEAR

GRADE

LINER NOTES

ARTIST

LABEL

ALBUM

COUNTRY

CATALOG NO.

YEAR

GRADE

LINER NOTES

ARTIST

LABEL

ALBUM

COUNTRY

CATALOG NO.

YEAR

GRADE

LINER NOTES

ARTIST

LABEL

ALBUM

COUNTRY

CATALOG NO.

YEAR

GRADE

LINER NOTES

ARTIST	LABEL	
ALBUM	COUNTRY	
CATALOG NO.	YEAR	GRADE

LINER NOTES

_____

_____

_____

_____

_____

ARTIST	LABEL	
ALBUM	COUNTRY	
CATALOG NO.	YEAR	GRADE

LINER NOTES

_____

_____

_____

_____

_____

ARTIST	LABEL	
ALBUM	COUNTRY	
CATALOG NO.	YEAR	GRADE

LINER NOTES

_____

_____

_____

_____

_____

ARTIST	LABEL	
ALBUM	COUNTRY	
CATALOG NO.	YEAR	GRADE

LINER NOTES

_____

_____

_____

_____

_____

ARTIST		LABEL	
ALBUM		COUNTRY	
CATALOG NO.		YEAR	GRADE

LINER NOTES

_____

_____

_____

_____

ARTIST		LABEL	
ALBUM		COUNTRY	
CATALOG NO.		YEAR	GRADE

LINER NOTES

_____

_____

_____

_____

ARTIST		LABEL	
ALBUM		COUNTRY	
CATALOG NO.		YEAR	GRADE

LINER NOTES

_____

_____

_____

_____

ARTIST		LABEL	
ALBUM		COUNTRY	
CATALOG NO.		YEAR	GRADE

LINER NOTES

_____

_____

_____

_____

ARTIST	LABEL	
ALBUM	COUNTRY	
CATALOG NO.	YEAR	GRADE

LINER NOTES

ARTIST	LABEL	
ALBUM	COUNTRY	
CATALOG NO.	YEAR	GRADE

LINER NOTES

ARTIST	LABEL	
ALBUM	COUNTRY	
CATALOG NO.	YEAR	GRADE

LINER NOTES

ARTIST	LABEL	
ALBUM	COUNTRY	
CATALOG NO.	YEAR	GRADE

LINER NOTES

ARTIST	LABEL	
ALBUM	COUNTRY	
CATALOG NO.	YEAR	GRADE

LINER NOTES

ARTIST	LABEL	
ALBUM	COUNTRY	
CATALOG NO.	YEAR	GRADE

LINER NOTES

ARTIST	LABEL	
ALBUM	COUNTRY	
CATALOG NO.	YEAR	GRADE

LINER NOTES

ARTIST	LABEL	
ALBUM	COUNTRY	
CATALOG NO.	YEAR	GRADE

LINER NOTES

ARTIST	LABEL	
ALBUM	COUNTRY	
CATALOG NO.	YEAR	GRADE

LINER NOTES

ARTIST	LABEL	
ALBUM	COUNTRY	
CATALOG NO.	YEAR	GRADE

LINER NOTES

ARTIST	LABEL	
ALBUM	COUNTRY	
CATALOG NO.	YEAR	GRADE

LINER NOTES

ARTIST	LABEL	
ALBUM	COUNTRY	
CATALOG NO.	YEAR	GRADE

LINER NOTES

ARTIST	LABEL	
ALBUM	COUNTRY	
CATALOG NO.	YEAR	GRADE

LINER NOTES

ARTIST	LABEL	
ALBUM	COUNTRY	
CATALOG NO.	YEAR	GRADE

LINER NOTES

ARTIST	LABEL	
ALBUM	COUNTRY	
CATALOG NO.	YEAR	GRADE

LINER NOTES

ARTIST	LABEL	
ALBUM	COUNTRY	
CATALOG NO.	YEAR	GRADE

LINER NOTES

ARTIST

LABEL

ALBUM

COUNTRY

CATALOG NO.

YEAR

GRADE

LINER NOTES

ARTIST

LABEL

ALBUM

COUNTRY

CATALOG NO.

YEAR

GRADE

LINER NOTES

ARTIST

LABEL

ALBUM

COUNTRY

CATALOG NO.

YEAR

GRADE

LINER NOTES

ARTIST

LABEL

ALBUM

COUNTRY

CATALOG NO.

YEAR

GRADE

LINER NOTES

ARTIST

LABEL

ALBUM

COUNTRY

CATALOG NO.

YEAR

GRADE

LINER NOTES

ARTIST

LABEL

ALBUM

COUNTRY

CATALOG NO.

YEAR

GRADE

LINER NOTES

ARTIST

LABEL

ALBUM

COUNTRY

CATALOG NO.

YEAR

GRADE

LINER NOTES

ARTIST

LABEL

ALBUM

COUNTRY

CATALOG NO.

YEAR

GRADE

LINER NOTES

ARTIST

ALBUM

CATALOG NO.

LINER NOTES

LABEL

COUNTRY

YEAR

GRADE

ARTIST

ALBUM

CATALOG NO.

LINER NOTES

LABEL

COUNTRY

YEAR

GRADE

ARTIST

ALBUM

CATALOG NO.

LINER NOTES

LABEL

COUNTRY

YEAR

GRADE

ARTIST

ALBUM

CATALOG NO.

LINER NOTES

LABEL

COUNTRY

YEAR

GRADE

ARTIST	LABEL	
ALBUM	COUNTRY	
CATALOG NO.	YEAR	GRADE

LINER NOTES

_____

_____

_____

_____

_____

ARTIST	LABEL	
ALBUM	COUNTRY	
CATALOG NO.	YEAR	GRADE

LINER NOTES

_____

_____

_____

_____

_____

ARTIST	LABEL	
ALBUM	COUNTRY	
CATALOG NO.	YEAR	GRADE

LINER NOTES

_____

_____

_____

_____

_____

ARTIST	LABEL	
ALBUM	COUNTRY	
CATALOG NO.	YEAR	GRADE

LINER NOTES

_____

_____

_____

_____

ARTIST   LABEL

ALBUM   COUNTRY

CATALOG NO.   YEAR   GRADE

LINER NOTES

ARTIST   LABEL

ALBUM   COUNTRY

CATALOG NO.   YEAR   GRADE

LINER NOTES

ARTIST   LABEL

ALBUM   COUNTRY

CATALOG NO.   YEAR   GRADE

LINER NOTES

ARTIST   LABEL

ALBUM   COUNTRY

CATALOG NO.   YEAR   GRADE

LINER NOTES

ARTIST

LABEL

ALBUM

COUNTRY

CATALOG NO.

YEAR

GRADE

LINER NOTES

ARTIST

LABEL

ALBUM

COUNTRY

CATALOG NO.

YEAR

GRADE

LINER NOTES

ARTIST

LABEL

ALBUM

COUNTRY

CATALOG NO.

YEAR

GRADE

LINER NOTES

ARTIST

LABEL

ALBUM

COUNTRY

CATALOG NO.

YEAR

GRADE

LINER NOTES

ARTIST	LABEL	
ALBUM	COUNTRY	
CATALOG NO.	YEAR	GRADE

LINER NOTES

ARTIST	LABEL	
ALBUM	COUNTRY	
CATALOG NO.	YEAR	GRADE

LINER NOTES

ARTIST	LABEL	
ALBUM	COUNTRY	
CATALOG NO.	YEAR	GRADE

LINER NOTES

ARTIST	LABEL	
ALBUM	COUNTRY	
CATALOG NO.	YEAR	GRADE

LINER NOTES

ARTIST

ALBUM

CATALOG NO.

LINER NOTES

LABEL

COUNTRY

YEAR | GRADE

ARTIST

ALBUM

CATALOG NO.

LINER NOTES

LABEL

COUNTRY

YEAR | GRADE

ARTIST

ALBUM

CATALOG NO.

LINER NOTES

LABEL

COUNTRY

YEAR | GRADE

ARTIST

ALBUM

CATALOG NO.

LINER NOTES

LABEL

COUNTRY

YEAR | GRADE

ARTIST	LABEL	
ALBUM	COUNTRY	
CATALOG NO.	YEAR	GRADE

LINER NOTES

ARTIST	LABEL	
ALBUM	COUNTRY	
CATALOG NO.	YEAR	GRADE

LINER NOTES

ARTIST	LABEL	
ALBUM	COUNTRY	
CATALOG NO.	YEAR	GRADE

LINER NOTES

ARTIST	LABEL	
ALBUM	COUNTRY	
CATALOG NO.	YEAR	GRADE

LINER NOTES

ARTIST	LABEL	
ALBUM	COUNTRY	
CATALOG NO.	YEAR	GRADE

LINER NOTES

ARTIST	LABEL	
ALBUM	COUNTRY	
CATALOG NO.	YEAR	GRADE

LINER NOTES

ARTIST	LABEL	
ALBUM	COUNTRY	
CATALOG NO.	YEAR	GRADE

LINER NOTES

ARTIST	LABEL	
ALBUM	COUNTRY	
CATALOG NO.	YEAR	GRADE

LINER NOTES

ARTIST	LABEL	
ALBUM	COUNTRY	
CATALOG NO.	YEAR	GRADE

LINER NOTES

ARTIST	LABEL	
ALBUM	COUNTRY	
CATALOG NO.	YEAR	GRADE

LINER NOTES

ARTIST	LABEL	
ALBUM	COUNTRY	
CATALOG NO.	YEAR	GRADE

LINER NOTES

ARTIST	LABEL	
ALBUM	COUNTRY	
CATALOG NO.	YEAR	GRADE

LINER NOTES

ARTIST	LABEL	
ALBUM	COUNTRY	
CATALOG NO.	YEAR	GRADE

LINER NOTES

ARTIST	LABEL	
ALBUM	COUNTRY	
CATALOG NO.	YEAR	GRADE

LINER NOTES

ARTIST	LABEL	
ALBUM	COUNTRY	
CATALOG NO.	YEAR	GRADE

LINER NOTES

ARTIST	LABEL	
ALBUM	COUNTRY	
CATALOG NO.	YEAR	GRADE

LINER NOTES

ARTIST	LABEL	
ALBUM	COUNTRY	
CATALOG NO.	YEAR	GRADE

LINER NOTES

ARTIST	LABEL	
ALBUM	COUNTRY	
CATALOG NO.	YEAR	GRADE

LINER NOTES

ARTIST	LABEL	
ALBUM	COUNTRY	
CATALOG NO.	YEAR	GRADE

LINER NOTES

ARTIST	LABEL	
ALBUM	COUNTRY	
CATALOG NO.	YEAR	GRADE

LINER NOTES

ARTIST   LABEL

ALBUM   COUNTRY

CATALOG NO.   YEAR   GRADE

LINER NOTES

ARTIST   LABEL

ALBUM   COUNTRY

CATALOG NO.   YEAR   GRADE

LINER NOTES

ARTIST   LABEL

ALBUM   COUNTRY

CATALOG NO.   YEAR   GRADE

LINER NOTES

ARTIST   LABEL

ALBUM   COUNTRY

CATALOG NO.   YEAR   GRADE

LINER NOTES

ARTIST | LABEL

ALBUM | COUNTRY

CATALOG NO. | YEAR | GRADE

LINER NOTES

ARTIST | LABEL

ALBUM | COUNTRY

CATALOG NO. | YEAR | GRADE

LINER NOTES

ARTIST | LABEL

ALBUM | COUNTRY

CATALOG NO. | YEAR | GRADE

LINER NOTES

ARTIST | LABEL

ALBUM | COUNTRY

CATALOG NO. | YEAR | GRADE

LINER NOTES

ARTIST	LABEL	
ALBUM	COUNTRY	
CATALOG NO.	YEAR	GRADE

LINER NOTES

ARTIST	LABEL	
ALBUM	COUNTRY	
CATALOG NO.	YEAR	GRADE

LINER NOTES

ARTIST	LABEL	
ALBUM	COUNTRY	
CATALOG NO.	YEAR	GRADE

LINER NOTES

ARTIST	LABEL	
ALBUM	COUNTRY	
CATALOG NO.	YEAR	GRADE

LINER NOTES

CATEGORY

ARTIST	LABEL	
ALBUM	COUNTRY	
CATALOG NO.	YEAR	GRADE

LINER NOTES

ARTIST	LABEL	
ALBUM	COUNTRY	
CATALOG NO.	YEAR	GRADE

LINER NOTES

ARTIST	LABEL	
ALBUM	COUNTRY	
CATALOG NO.	YEAR	GRADE

LINER NOTES

ARTIST	LABEL	
ALBUM	COUNTRY	
CATALOG NO.	YEAR	GRADE

LINER NOTES

ARTIST	LABEL	
ALBUM	COUNTRY	
CATALOG NO.	YEAR	GRADE

LINER NOTES

ARTIST	LABEL	
ALBUM	COUNTRY	
CATALOG NO.	YEAR	GRADE

LINER NOTES

ARTIST	LABEL	
ALBUM	COUNTRY	
CATALOG NO.	YEAR	GRADE

LINER NOTES

ARTIST	LABEL	
ALBUM	COUNTRY	
CATALOG NO.	YEAR	GRADE

LINER NOTES

ARTIST	LABEL	
ALBUM	COUNTRY	
CATALOG NO.	YEAR	GRADE

LINER NOTES

ARTIST	LABEL	
ALBUM	COUNTRY	
CATALOG NO.	YEAR	GRADE

LINER NOTES

ARTIST	LABEL	
ALBUM	COUNTRY	
CATALOG NO.	YEAR	GRADE

LINER NOTES

ARTIST	LABEL	
ALBUM	COUNTRY	
CATALOG NO.	YEAR	GRADE

LINER NOTES

ARTIST	LABEL	
ALBUM	COUNTRY	
CATALOG NO.	YEAR	GRADE

LINER NOTES

ARTIST	LABEL	
ALBUM	COUNTRY	
CATALOG NO.	YEAR	GRADE

LINER NOTES

ARTIST	LABEL	
ALBUM	COUNTRY	
CATALOG NO.	YEAR	GRADE

LINER NOTES

ARTIST	LABEL	
ALBUM	COUNTRY	
CATALOG NO.	YEAR	GRADE

LINER NOTES

ARTIST	LABEL	
ALBUM	COUNTRY	
CATALOG NO.	YEAR	GRADE

LINER NOTES

_____

_____

_____

_____

ARTIST	LABEL	
ALBUM	COUNTRY	
CATALOG NO.	YEAR	GRADE

LINER NOTES

_____

_____

_____

_____

ARTIST	LABEL	
ALBUM	COUNTRY	
CATALOG NO.	YEAR	GRADE

LINER NOTES

_____

_____

_____

_____

ARTIST	LABEL	
ALBUM	COUNTRY	
CATALOG NO.	YEAR	GRADE

LINER NOTES

_____

_____

_____

_____

ARTIST		LABEL	
ALBUM		COUNTRY	
CATALOG NO.		YEAR	GRADE

LINER NOTES

ARTIST		LABEL	
ALBUM		COUNTRY	
CATALOG NO.		YEAR	GRADE

LINER NOTES

ARTIST		LABEL	
ALBUM		COUNTRY	
CATALOG NO.		YEAR	GRADE

LINER NOTES

ARTIST		LABEL	
ALBUM		COUNTRY	
CATALOG NO.		YEAR	GRADE

LINER NOTES

CATEGORY

ARTIST		LABEL	
ALBUM		COUNTRY	
CATALOG NO.		YEAR	GRADE

LINER NOTES

ARTIST		LABEL	
ALBUM		COUNTRY	
CATALOG NO.		YEAR	GRADE

LINER NOTES

ARTIST		LABEL	
ALBUM		COUNTRY	
CATALOG NO.		YEAR	GRADE

LINER NOTES

ARTIST		LABEL	
ALBUM		COUNTRY	
CATALOG NO.		YEAR	GRADE

LINER NOTES

ARTIST

ALBUM

CATALOG NO.

LINER NOTES

LABEL

COUNTRY

YEAR | GRADE

ARTIST

ALBUM

CATALOG NO.

LINER NOTES

LABEL

COUNTRY

YEAR | GRADE

ARTIST

ALBUM

CATALOG NO.

LINER NOTES

LABEL

COUNTRY

YEAR | GRADE

ARTIST

ALBUM

CATALOG NO.

LINER NOTES

LABEL

COUNTRY

YEAR | GRADE

ARTIST		LABEL	
ALBUM		COUNTRY	
CATALOG NO.		YEAR	GRADE

LINER NOTES

_____

_____

_____

_____

ARTIST		LABEL	
ALBUM		COUNTRY	
CATALOG NO.		YEAR	GRADE

LINER NOTES

_____

_____

_____

_____

ARTIST		LABEL	
ALBUM		COUNTRY	
CATALOG NO.		YEAR	GRADE

LINER NOTES

_____

_____

_____

_____

ARTIST		LABEL	
ALBUM		COUNTRY	
CATALOG NO.		YEAR	GRADE

LINER NOTES

_____

_____

_____

_____

ARTIST | LABEL

ALBUM | COUNTRY

CATALOG NO. | YEAR | GRADE

LINER NOTES

ARTIST | LABEL

ALBUM | COUNTRY

CATALOG NO. | YEAR | GRADE

LINER NOTES

ARTIST | LABEL

ALBUM | COUNTRY

CATALOG NO. | YEAR | GRADE

LINER NOTES

ARTIST | LABEL

ALBUM | COUNTRY

CATALOG NO. | YEAR | GRADE

LINER NOTES

ARTIST		LABEL	
ALBUM		COUNTRY	
CATALOG NO.		YEAR	GRADE

LINER NOTES

ARTIST		LABEL	
ALBUM		COUNTRY	
CATALOG NO.		YEAR	GRADE

LINER NOTES

ARTIST		LABEL	
ALBUM		COUNTRY	
CATALOG NO.		YEAR	GRADE

LINER NOTES

ARTIST		LABEL	
ALBUM		COUNTRY	
CATALOG NO.		YEAR	GRADE

LINER NOTES

ARTIST	LABEL	
ALBUM	COUNTRY	
CATALOG NO.	YEAR	GRADE

LINER NOTES

_____
_____
_____
_____
_____

ARTIST	LABEL	
ALBUM	COUNTRY	
CATALOG NO.	YEAR	GRADE

LINER NOTES

_____
_____
_____
_____
_____

ARTIST	LABEL	
ALBUM	COUNTRY	
CATALOG NO.	YEAR	GRADE

LINER NOTES

_____
_____
_____
_____
_____

ARTIST	LABEL	
ALBUM	COUNTRY	
CATALOG NO.	YEAR	GRADE

LINER NOTES

_____
_____
_____
_____

ARTIST	LABEL	
ALBUM	COUNTRY	
CATALOG NO.	YEAR	GRADE

LINER NOTES

ARTIST	LABEL	
ALBUM	COUNTRY	
CATALOG NO.	YEAR	GRADE

LINER NOTES

ARTIST	LABEL	
ALBUM	COUNTRY	
CATALOG NO.	YEAR	GRADE

LINER NOTES

ARTIST	LABEL	
ALBUM	COUNTRY	
CATALOG NO.	YEAR	GRADE

LINER NOTES

ARTIST

LABEL

ALBUM

COUNTRY

CATALOG NO.

YEAR

GRADE

LINER NOTES

ARTIST

LABEL

ALBUM

COUNTRY

CATALOG NO.

YEAR

GRADE

LINER NOTES

ARTIST

LABEL

ALBUM

COUNTRY

CATALOG NO.

YEAR

GRADE

LINER NOTES

ARTIST

LABEL

ALBUM

COUNTRY

CATALOG NO.

YEAR

GRADE

LINER NOTES

CATEGORY

ARTIST | LABEL
ALBUM | COUNTRY
CATALOG NO. | YEAR | GRADE
LINER NOTES

ARTIST | LABEL
ALBUM | COUNTRY
CATALOG NO. | YEAR | GRADE
LINER NOTES

ARTIST | LABEL
ALBUM | COUNTRY
CATALOG NO. | YEAR | GRADE
LINER NOTES

ARTIST | LABEL
ALBUM | COUNTRY
CATALOG NO. | YEAR | GRADE
LINER NOTES

ARTIST	LABEL	
ALBUM	COUNTRY	
CATALOG NO.	YEAR	GRADE

LINER NOTES

ARTIST	LABEL	
ALBUM	COUNTRY	
CATALOG NO.	YEAR	GRADE

LINER NOTES

ARTIST	LABEL	
ALBUM	COUNTRY	
CATALOG NO.	YEAR	GRADE

LINER NOTES

ARTIST	LABEL	
ALBUM	COUNTRY	
CATALOG NO.	YEAR	GRADE

LINER NOTES

ARTIST

LABEL

ALBUM

COUNTRY

CATALOG NO.

YEAR

GRADE

LINER NOTES

ARTIST

LABEL

ALBUM

COUNTRY

CATALOG NO.

YEAR

GRADE

LINER NOTES

ARTIST

LABEL

ALBUM

COUNTRY

CATALOG NO.

YEAR

GRADE

LINER NOTES

ARTIST

LABEL

ALBUM

COUNTRY

CATALOG NO.

YEAR

GRADE

LINER NOTES

ARTIST

ALBUM

CATALOG NO.

LINER NOTES

LABEL

COUNTRY

YEAR | GRADE

ARTIST

ALBUM

CATALOG NO.

LINER NOTES

LABEL

COUNTRY

YEAR | GRADE

ARTIST

ALBUM

CATALOG NO.

LINER NOTES

LABEL

COUNTRY

YEAR | GRADE

ARTIST

ALBUM

CATALOG NO.

LINER NOTES

LABEL

COUNTRY

YEAR | GRADE

ARTIST

LABEL

ALBUM

COUNTRY

CATALOG NO.

YEAR

GRADE

LINER NOTES

ARTIST

LABEL

ALBUM

COUNTRY

CATALOG NO.

YEAR

GRADE

LINER NOTES

ARTIST

LABEL

ALBUM

COUNTRY

CATALOG NO.

YEAR

GRADE

LINER NOTES

ARTIST

LABEL

ALBUM

COUNTRY

CATALOG NO.

YEAR

GRADE

LINER NOTES

ARTIST	LABEL	
ALBUM	COUNTRY	
CATALOG NO.	YEAR	GRADE

LINER NOTES

ARTIST	LABEL	
ALBUM	COUNTRY	
CATALOG NO.	YEAR	GRADE

LINER NOTES

ARTIST	LABEL	
ALBUM	COUNTRY	
CATALOG NO.	YEAR	GRADE

LINER NOTES

ARTIST	LABEL	
ALBUM	COUNTRY	
CATALOG NO.	YEAR	GRADE

LINER NOTES

ARTIST	LABEL	
ALBUM	COUNTRY	
CATALOG NO.	YEAR	GRADE

LINER NOTES

ARTIST	LABEL	
ALBUM	COUNTRY	
CATALOG NO.	YEAR	GRADE

LINER NOTES

ARTIST	LABEL	
ALBUM	COUNTRY	
CATALOG NO.	YEAR	GRADE

LINER NOTES

ARTIST	LABEL	
ALBUM	COUNTRY	
CATALOG NO.	YEAR	GRADE

LINER NOTES

ARTIST

LABEL

ALBUM

COUNTRY

CATALOG NO.

YEAR

GRADE

LINER NOTES

ARTIST

LABEL

ALBUM

COUNTRY

CATALOG NO.

YEAR

GRADE

LINER NOTES

ARTIST

LABEL

ALBUM

COUNTRY

CATALOG NO.

YEAR

GRADE

LINER NOTES

ARTIST

LABEL

ALBUM

COUNTRY

CATALOG NO.

YEAR

GRADE

LINER NOTES

ARTIST	LABEL	
ALBUM	COUNTRY	
CATALOG NO.	YEAR	GRADE

LINER NOTES

ARTIST	LABEL	
ALBUM	COUNTRY	
CATALOG NO.	YEAR	GRADE

LINER NOTES

ARTIST	LABEL	
ALBUM	COUNTRY	
CATALOG NO.	YEAR	GRADE

LINER NOTES

ARTIST	LABEL	
ALBUM	COUNTRY	
CATALOG NO.	YEAR	GRADE

LINER NOTES

ARTIST

ALBUM

CATALOG NO.

LINER NOTES

LABEL

COUNTRY

YEAR | GRADE

ARTIST

ALBUM

CATALOG NO.

LINER NOTES

LABEL

COUNTRY

YEAR | GRADE

ARTIST

ALBUM

CATALOG NO.

LINER NOTES

LABEL

COUNTRY

YEAR | GRADE

ARTIST

ALBUM

CATALOG NO.

LINER NOTES

LABEL

COUNTRY

YEAR | GRADE

ARTIST   LABEL

ALBUM   COUNTRY

CATALOG NO.   YEAR   GRADE

LINER NOTES

ARTIST   LABEL

ALBUM   COUNTRY

CATALOG NO.   YEAR   GRADE

LINER NOTES

ARTIST   LABEL

ALBUM   COUNTRY

CATALOG NO.   YEAR   GRADE

LINER NOTES

ARTIST   LABEL

ALBUM   COUNTRY

CATALOG NO.   YEAR   GRADE

LINER NOTES

ARTIST

LABEL

ALBUM

COUNTRY

CATALOG NO.

YEAR

GRADE

LINER NOTES

ARTIST

LABEL

ALBUM

COUNTRY

CATALOG NO.

YEAR

GRADE

LINER NOTES

ARTIST

LABEL

ALBUM

COUNTRY

CATALOG NO.

YEAR

GRADE

LINER NOTES

ARTIST

LABEL

ALBUM

COUNTRY

CATALOG NO.

YEAR

GRADE

LINER NOTES

ARTIST | LABEL
ALBUM | COUNTRY
CATALOG NO. | YEAR | GRADE

LINER NOTES

ARTIST | LABEL
ALBUM | COUNTRY
CATALOG NO. | YEAR | GRADE

LINER NOTES

ARTIST | LABEL
ALBUM | COUNTRY
CATALOG NO. | YEAR | GRADE

LINER NOTES

ARTIST | LABEL
ALBUM | COUNTRY
CATALOG NO. | YEAR | GRADE

LINER NOTES

ARTIST

LABEL

ALBUM

COUNTRY

CATALOG NO.

YEAR

GRADE

LINER NOTES

ARTIST

LABEL

ALBUM

COUNTRY

CATALOG NO.

YEAR

GRADE

LINER NOTES

ARTIST

LABEL

ALBUM

COUNTRY

CATALOG NO.

YEAR

GRADE

LINER NOTES

ARTIST

LABEL

ALBUM

COUNTRY

CATALOG NO.

YEAR

GRADE

LINER NOTES

ARTIST | LABEL
ALBUM | COUNTRY
CATALOG NO. | YEAR | GRADE

LINER NOTES

ARTIST | LABEL
ALBUM | COUNTRY
CATALOG NO. | YEAR | GRADE

LINER NOTES

ARTIST | LABEL
ALBUM | COUNTRY
CATALOG NO. | YEAR | GRADE

LINER NOTES

ARTIST | LABEL
ALBUM | COUNTRY
CATALOG NO. | YEAR | GRADE

LINER NOTES

ARTIST	LABEL	
ALBUM	COUNTRY	
CATALOG NO.	YEAR	GRADE

LINER NOTES

ARTIST	LABEL	
ALBUM	COUNTRY	
CATALOG NO.	YEAR	GRADE

LINER NOTES

ARTIST	LABEL	
ALBUM	COUNTRY	
CATALOG NO.	YEAR	GRADE

LINER NOTES

ARTIST	LABEL	
ALBUM	COUNTRY	
CATALOG NO.	YEAR	GRADE

LINER NOTES

ARTIST	LABEL	
ALBUM	COUNTRY	
CATALOG NO.	YEAR	GRADE

LINER NOTES

ARTIST	LABEL	
ALBUM	COUNTRY	
CATALOG NO.	YEAR	GRADE

LINER NOTES

ARTIST	LABEL	
ALBUM	COUNTRY	
CATALOG NO.	YEAR	GRADE

LINER NOTES

ARTIST	LABEL	
ALBUM	COUNTRY	
CATALOG NO.	YEAR	GRADE

LINER NOTES

ARTIST

LABEL

ALBUM

COUNTRY

CATALOG NO.

YEAR

GRADE

LINER NOTES

ARTIST

LABEL

ALBUM

COUNTRY

CATALOG NO.

YEAR

GRADE

LINER NOTES

ARTIST

LABEL

ALBUM

COUNTRY

CATALOG NO.

YEAR

GRADE

LINER NOTES

ARTIST

LABEL

ALBUM

COUNTRY

CATALOG NO.

YEAR

GRADE

LINER NOTES

ARTIST		LABEL	
ALBUM		COUNTRY	
CATALOG NO.		YEAR	GRADE

LINER NOTES

ARTIST		LABEL	
ALBUM		COUNTRY	
CATALOG NO.		YEAR	GRADE

LINER NOTES

ARTIST		LABEL	
ALBUM		COUNTRY	
CATALOG NO.		YEAR	GRADE

LINER NOTES

ARTIST		LABEL	
ALBUM		COUNTRY	
CATALOG NO.		YEAR	GRADE

LINER NOTES

ARTIST | LABEL

ALBUM | COUNTRY

CATALOG NO. | YEAR | GRADE

LINER NOTES

ARTIST | LABEL

ALBUM | COUNTRY

CATALOG NO. | YEAR | GRADE

LINER NOTES

ARTIST | LABEL

ALBUM | COUNTRY

CATALOG NO. | YEAR | GRADE

LINER NOTES

ARTIST | LABEL

ALBUM | COUNTRY

CATALOG NO. | YEAR | GRADE

LINER NOTES

ARTIST

LABEL

ALBUM

COUNTRY

CATALOG NO.

YEAR

GRADE

LINER NOTES

ARTIST

LABEL

ALBUM

COUNTRY

CATALOG NO.

YEAR

GRADE

LINER NOTES

ARTIST

LABEL

ALBUM

COUNTRY

CATALOG NO.

YEAR

GRADE

LINER NOTES

ARTIST

LABEL

ALBUM

COUNTRY

CATALOG NO.

YEAR

GRADE

LINER NOTES

ARTIST

LABEL

ALBUM

COUNTRY

CATALOG NO.

YEAR

GRADE

LINER NOTES

ARTIST

LABEL

ALBUM

COUNTRY

CATALOG NO.

YEAR

GRADE

LINER NOTES

ARTIST

LABEL

ALBUM

COUNTRY

CATALOG NO.

YEAR

GRADE

LINER NOTES

ARTIST

LABEL

ALBUM

COUNTRY

CATALOG NO.

YEAR

GRADE

LINER NOTES

ARTIST | LABEL

ALBUM | COUNTRY

CATALOG NO. | YEAR | GRADE

LINER NOTES

ARTIST | LABEL

ALBUM | COUNTRY

CATALOG NO. | YEAR | GRADE

LINER NOTES

ARTIST | LABEL

ALBUM | COUNTRY

CATALOG NO. | YEAR | GRADE

LINER NOTES

ARTIST | LABEL

ALBUM | COUNTRY

CATALOG NO. | YEAR | GRADE

LINER NOTES

ARTIST

LABEL

ALBUM

COUNTRY

CATALOG NO.

YEAR

GRADE

LINER NOTES

ARTIST

LABEL

ALBUM

COUNTRY

CATALOG NO.

YEAR

GRADE

LINER NOTES

ARTIST

LABEL

ALBUM

COUNTRY

CATALOG NO.

YEAR

GRADE

LINER NOTES

ARTIST

LABEL

ALBUM

COUNTRY

CATALOG NO.

YEAR

GRADE

LINER NOTES

ARTIST

LABEL

ALBUM

COUNTRY

CATALOG NO.

YEAR

GRADE

LINER NOTES

ARTIST

LABEL

ALBUM

COUNTRY

CATALOG NO.

YEAR

GRADE

LINER NOTES

ARTIST

LABEL

ALBUM

COUNTRY

CATALOG NO.

YEAR

GRADE

LINER NOTES

ARTIST

LABEL

ALBUM

COUNTRY

CATALOG NO.

YEAR

GRADE

LINER NOTES

ARTIST	LABEL	
ALBUM	COUNTRY	
CATALOG NO.	YEAR	GRADE

LINER NOTES

ARTIST	LABEL	
ALBUM	COUNTRY	
CATALOG NO.	YEAR	GRADE

LINER NOTES

ARTIST	LABEL	
ALBUM	COUNTRY	
CATALOG NO.	YEAR	GRADE

LINER NOTES

ARTIST	LABEL	
ALBUM	COUNTRY	
CATALOG NO.	YEAR	GRADE

LINER NOTES

ARTIST	LABEL	
ALBUM	COUNTRY	
CATALOG NO.	YEAR	GRADE

LINER NOTES

_____

_____

_____

_____

ARTIST	LABEL	
ALBUM	COUNTRY	
CATALOG NO.	YEAR	GRADE

LINER NOTES

_____

_____

_____

_____

ARTIST	LABEL	
ALBUM	COUNTRY	
CATALOG NO.	YEAR	GRADE

LINER NOTES

_____

_____

_____

_____

ARTIST	LABEL	
ALBUM	COUNTRY	
CATALOG NO.	YEAR	GRADE

LINER NOTES

_____

_____

_____

_____

ARTIST	LABEL	
ALBUM	COUNTRY	
CATALOG NO.	YEAR	GRADE

LINER NOTES

ARTIST	LABEL	
ALBUM	COUNTRY	
CATALOG NO.	YEAR	GRADE

LINER NOTES

ARTIST	LABEL	
ALBUM	COUNTRY	
CATALOG NO.	YEAR	GRADE

LINER NOTES

ARTIST	LABEL	
ALBUM	COUNTRY	
CATALOG NO.	YEAR	GRADE

LINER NOTES

CATEGORY

ARTIST	LABEL	
ALBUM	COUNTRY	
CATALOG NO.	YEAR	GRADE

LINER NOTES

ARTIST	LABEL	
ALBUM	COUNTRY	
CATALOG NO.	YEAR	GRADE

LINER NOTES

ARTIST	LABEL	
ALBUM	COUNTRY	
CATALOG NO.	YEAR	GRADE

LINER NOTES

ARTIST	LABEL	
ALBUM	COUNTRY	
CATALOG NO.	YEAR	GRADE

LINER NOTES

ARTIST	LABEL	
ALBUM	COUNTRY	
CATALOG NO.	YEAR	GRADE

LINER NOTES

ARTIST	LABEL	
ALBUM	COUNTRY	
CATALOG NO.	YEAR	GRADE

LINER NOTES

ARTIST	LABEL	
ALBUM	COUNTRY	
CATALOG NO.	YEAR	GRADE

LINER NOTES

ARTIST	LABEL	
ALBUM	COUNTRY	
CATALOG NO.	YEAR	GRADE

LINER NOTES

ARTIST	LABEL	
ALBUM	COUNTRY	
CATALOG NO.	YEAR	GRADE

LINER NOTES

ARTIST	LABEL	
ALBUM	COUNTRY	
CATALOG NO.	YEAR	GRADE

LINER NOTES

ARTIST	LABEL	
ALBUM	COUNTRY	
CATALOG NO.	YEAR	GRADE

LINER NOTES

ARTIST	LABEL	
ALBUM	COUNTRY	
CATALOG NO.	YEAR	GRADE

LINER NOTES

ARTIST

LABEL

ALBUM

COUNTRY

CATALOG NO.

YEAR

GRADE

LINER NOTES

ARTIST

LABEL

ALBUM

COUNTRY

CATALOG NO.

YEAR

GRADE

LINER NOTES

ARTIST

LABEL

ALBUM

COUNTRY

CATALOG NO.

YEAR

GRADE

LINER NOTES

ARTIST

LABEL

ALBUM

COUNTRY

CATALOG NO.

YEAR

GRADE

LINER NOTES

CATEGORY

ARTIST	LABEL	
ALBUM	COUNTRY	
CATALOG NO.	YEAR	GRADE

LINER NOTES

ARTIST	LABEL	
ALBUM	COUNTRY	
CATALOG NO.	YEAR	GRADE

LINER NOTES

ARTIST	LABEL	
ALBUM	COUNTRY	
CATALOG NO.	YEAR	GRADE

LINER NOTES

ARTIST	LABEL	
ALBUM	COUNTRY	
CATALOG NO.	YEAR	GRADE

LINER NOTES

ARTIST

LABEL

ALBUM

COUNTRY

CATALOG NO.

YEAR

GRADE

LINER NOTES

ARTIST

LABEL

ALBUM

COUNTRY

CATALOG NO.

YEAR

GRADE

LINER NOTES

ARTIST

LABEL

ALBUM

COUNTRY

CATALOG NO.

YEAR

GRADE

LINER NOTES

ARTIST

LABEL

ALBUM

COUNTRY

CATALOG NO.

YEAR

GRADE

LINER NOTES

ARTIST	LABEL	
ALBUM	COUNTRY	
CATALOG NO.	YEAR	GRADE

LINER NOTES

ARTIST	LABEL	
ALBUM	COUNTRY	
CATALOG NO.	YEAR	GRADE

LINER NOTES

ARTIST	LABEL	
ALBUM	COUNTRY	
CATALOG NO.	YEAR	GRADE

LINER NOTES

ARTIST	LABEL	
ALBUM	COUNTRY	
CATALOG NO.	YEAR	GRADE

LINER NOTES

ARTIST		LABEL	
ALBUM		COUNTRY	
CATALOG NO.		YEAR	GRADE

LINER NOTES

ARTIST		LABEL	
ALBUM		COUNTRY	
CATALOG NO.		YEAR	GRADE

LINER NOTES

ARTIST		LABEL	
ALBUM		COUNTRY	
CATALOG NO.		YEAR	GRADE

LINER NOTES

ARTIST		LABEL	
ALBUM		COUNTRY	
CATALOG NO.		YEAR	GRADE

LINER NOTES

ARTIST	LABEL	
ALBUM	COUNTRY	
CATALOG NO.	YEAR	GRADE

LINER NOTES

ARTIST	LABEL	
ALBUM	COUNTRY	
CATALOG NO.	YEAR	GRADE

LINER NOTES

ARTIST	LABEL	
ALBUM	COUNTRY	
CATALOG NO.	YEAR	GRADE

LINER NOTES

ARTIST	LABEL	
ALBUM	COUNTRY	
CATALOG NO.	YEAR	GRADE

LINER NOTES

ARTIST	LABEL	
ALBUM	COUNTRY	
CATALOG NO.	YEAR	GRADE

LINER NOTES

ARTIST	LABEL	
ALBUM	COUNTRY	
CATALOG NO.	YEAR	GRADE

LINER NOTES

ARTIST	LABEL	
ALBUM	COUNTRY	
CATALOG NO.	YEAR	GRADE

LINER NOTES

ARTIST	LABEL	
ALBUM	COUNTRY	
CATALOG NO.	YEAR	GRADE

LINER NOTES

ARTIST	LABEL	
ALBUM	COUNTRY	
CATALOG NO.	YEAR	GRADE

LINER NOTES

_____
_____
_____
_____
_____

ARTIST	LABEL	
ALBUM	COUNTRY	
CATALOG NO.	YEAR	GRADE

LINER NOTES

_____
_____
_____
_____
_____

ARTIST	LABEL	
ALBUM	COUNTRY	
CATALOG NO.	YEAR	GRADE

LINER NOTES

_____
_____
_____
_____
_____

ARTIST	LABEL	
ALBUM	COUNTRY	
CATALOG NO.	YEAR	GRADE

LINER NOTES

_____
_____
_____
_____

ARTIST	LABEL	
ALBUM	COUNTRY	
CATALOG NO.	YEAR	GRADE

LINER NOTES

_____

_____

_____

_____

ARTIST	LABEL	
ALBUM	COUNTRY	
CATALOG NO.	YEAR	GRADE

LINER NOTES

_____

_____

_____

_____

ARTIST	LABEL	
ALBUM	COUNTRY	
CATALOG NO.	YEAR	GRADE

LINER NOTES

_____

_____

_____

_____

ARTIST	LABEL	
ALBUM	COUNTRY	
CATALOG NO.	YEAR	GRADE

LINER NOTES

_____

_____

_____

_____

ARTIST	LABEL	
ALBUM	COUNTRY	
CATALOG NO.	YEAR	GRADE

LINER NOTES

ARTIST	LABEL	
ALBUM	COUNTRY	
CATALOG NO.	YEAR	GRADE

LINER NOTES

ARTIST	LABEL	
ALBUM	COUNTRY	
CATALOG NO.	YEAR	GRADE

LINER NOTES

ARTIST	LABEL	
ALBUM	COUNTRY	
CATALOG NO.	YEAR	GRADE

LINER NOTES

ARTIST

LABEL

ALBUM

COUNTRY

CATALOG NO.

YEAR

GRADE

LINER NOTES

ARTIST

LABEL

ALBUM

COUNTRY

CATALOG NO.

YEAR

GRADE

LINER NOTES

ARTIST

LABEL

ALBUM

COUNTRY

CATALOG NO.

YEAR

GRADE

LINER NOTES

ARTIST

LABEL

ALBUM

COUNTRY

CATALOG NO.

YEAR

GRADE

LINER NOTES

ARTIST	LABEL	
ALBUM	COUNTRY	
CATALOG NO.	YEAR	GRADE

LINER NOTES

ARTIST	LABEL	
ALBUM	COUNTRY	
CATALOG NO.	YEAR	GRADE

LINER NOTES

ARTIST	LABEL	
ALBUM	COUNTRY	
CATALOG NO.	YEAR	GRADE

LINER NOTES

ARTIST	LABEL	
ALBUM	COUNTRY	
CATALOG NO.	YEAR	GRADE

LINER NOTES

ARTIST	LABEL	
ALBUM	COUNTRY	
CATALOG NO.	YEAR	GRADE

LINER NOTES

ARTIST	LABEL	
ALBUM	COUNTRY	
CATALOG NO.	YEAR	GRADE

LINER NOTES

ARTIST	LABEL	
ALBUM	COUNTRY	
CATALOG NO.	YEAR	GRADE

LINER NOTES

ARTIST	LABEL	
ALBUM	COUNTRY	
CATALOG NO.	YEAR	GRADE

LINER NOTES

ARTIST	LABEL	
ALBUM	COUNTRY	
CATALOG NO.	YEAR	GRADE

LINER NOTES

ARTIST	LABEL	
ALBUM	COUNTRY	
CATALOG NO.	YEAR	GRADE

LINER NOTES

ARTIST	LABEL	
ALBUM	COUNTRY	
CATALOG NO.	YEAR	GRADE

LINER NOTES

ARTIST	LABEL	
ALBUM	COUNTRY	
CATALOG NO.	YEAR	GRADE

LINER NOTES

ARTIST

LABEL

ALBUM

COUNTRY

CATALOG NO.

YEAR

GRADE

LINER NOTES

ARTIST

LABEL

ALBUM

COUNTRY

CATALOG NO.

YEAR

GRADE

LINER NOTES

ARTIST

LABEL

ALBUM

COUNTRY

CATALOG NO.

YEAR

GRADE

LINER NOTES

ARTIST

LABEL

ALBUM

COUNTRY

CATALOG NO.

YEAR

GRADE

LINER NOTES

ARTIST | LABEL

ALBUM | COUNTRY

CATALOG NO. | YEAR | GRADE

LINER NOTES

ARTIST | LABEL

ALBUM | COUNTRY

CATALOG NO. | YEAR | GRADE

LINER NOTES

ARTIST | LABEL

ALBUM | COUNTRY

CATALOG NO. | YEAR | GRADE

LINER NOTES

ARTIST | LABEL

ALBUM | COUNTRY

CATALOG NO. | YEAR | GRADE

LINER NOTES

ARTIST	LABEL	
ALBUM	COUNTRY	
CATALOG NO.	YEAR	GRADE

LINER NOTES

ARTIST	LABEL	
ALBUM	COUNTRY	
CATALOG NO.	YEAR	GRADE

LINER NOTES

ARTIST	LABEL	
ALBUM	COUNTRY	
CATALOG NO.	YEAR	GRADE

LINER NOTES

ARTIST	LABEL	
ALBUM	COUNTRY	
CATALOG NO.	YEAR	GRADE

LINER NOTES

ARTIST	LABEL	
ALBUM	COUNTRY	
CATALOG NO.	YEAR	GRADE

LINER NOTES

ARTIST	LABEL	
ALBUM	COUNTRY	
CATALOG NO.	YEAR	GRADE

LINER NOTES

ARTIST	LABEL	
ALBUM	COUNTRY	
CATALOG NO.	YEAR	GRADE

LINER NOTES

ARTIST	LABEL	
ALBUM	COUNTRY	
CATALOG NO.	YEAR	GRADE

LINER NOTES

ARTIST	LABEL	
ALBUM	COUNTRY	
CATALOG NO.	YEAR	GRADE

LINER NOTES

ARTIST	LABEL	
ALBUM	COUNTRY	
CATALOG NO.	YEAR	GRADE

LINER NOTES

ARTIST	LABEL	
ALBUM	COUNTRY	
CATALOG NO.	YEAR	GRADE

LINER NOTES

ARTIST	LABEL	
ALBUM	COUNTRY	
CATALOG NO.	YEAR	GRADE

LINER NOTES

CATEGORY

ARTIST	LABEL	
ALBUM	COUNTRY	
CATALOG NO.	YEAR	GRADE

LINER NOTES

ARTIST	LABEL	
ALBUM	COUNTRY	
CATALOG NO.	YEAR	GRADE

LINER NOTES

ARTIST	LABEL	
ALBUM	COUNTRY	
CATALOG NO.	YEAR	GRADE

LINER NOTES

ARTIST	LABEL	
ALBUM	COUNTRY	
CATALOG NO.	YEAR	GRADE

LINER NOTES

ARTIST

LABEL

ALBUM

COUNTRY

CATALOG NO.

YEAR

GRADE

LINER NOTES

ARTIST

LABEL

ALBUM

COUNTRY

CATALOG NO.

YEAR

GRADE

LINER NOTES

ARTIST

LABEL

ALBUM

COUNTRY

CATALOG NO.

YEAR

GRADE

LINER NOTES

ARTIST

LABEL

ALBUM

COUNTRY

CATALOG NO.

YEAR

GRADE

LINER NOTES

ARTIST	LABEL	
ALBUM	COUNTRY	
CATALOG NO.	YEAR	GRADE

LINER NOTES

_____

_____

_____

_____

ARTIST	LABEL	
ALBUM	COUNTRY	
CATALOG NO.	YEAR	GRADE

LINER NOTES

_____

_____

_____

_____

ARTIST	LABEL	
ALBUM	COUNTRY	
CATALOG NO.	YEAR	GRADE

LINER NOTES

_____

_____

_____

_____

ARTIST	LABEL	
ALBUM	COUNTRY	
CATALOG NO.	YEAR	GRADE

LINER NOTES

_____

_____

_____

_____

ARTIST	LABEL	
ALBUM	COUNTRY	
CATALOG NO.	YEAR	GRADE

LINER NOTES

_____

_____

_____

_____

ARTIST	LABEL	
ALBUM	COUNTRY	
CATALOG NO.	YEAR	GRADE

LINER NOTES

_____

_____

_____

_____

ARTIST	LABEL	
ALBUM	COUNTRY	
CATALOG NO.	YEAR	GRADE

LINER NOTES

_____

_____

_____

_____

ARTIST	LABEL	
ALBUM	COUNTRY	
CATALOG NO.	YEAR	GRADE

LINER NOTES

_____

_____

_____

_____

ARTIST	LABEL	
ALBUM	COUNTRY	
CATALOG NO.	YEAR	GRADE

LINER NOTES

ARTIST	LABEL	
ALBUM	COUNTRY	
CATALOG NO.	YEAR	GRADE

LINER NOTES

ARTIST	LABEL	
ALBUM	COUNTRY	
CATALOG NO.	YEAR	GRADE

LINER NOTES

ARTIST	LABEL	
ALBUM	COUNTRY	
CATALOG NO.	YEAR	GRADE

LINER NOTES

ARTIST

LABEL

ALBUM

COUNTRY

CATALOG NO.

YEAR

GRADE

LINER NOTES

ARTIST

LABEL

ALBUM

COUNTRY

CATALOG NO.

YEAR

GRADE

LINER NOTES

ARTIST

LABEL

ALBUM

COUNTRY

CATALOG NO.

YEAR

GRADE

LINER NOTES

ARTIST

LABEL

ALBUM

COUNTRY

CATALOG NO.

YEAR

GRADE

LINER NOTES

ARTIST	LABEL	
ALBUM	COUNTRY	
CATALOG NO.	YEAR	GRADE

LINER NOTES

ARTIST	LABEL	
ALBUM	COUNTRY	
CATALOG NO.	YEAR	GRADE

LINER NOTES

ARTIST	LABEL	
ALBUM	COUNTRY	
CATALOG NO.	YEAR	GRADE

LINER NOTES

ARTIST	LABEL	
ALBUM	COUNTRY	
CATALOG NO.	YEAR	GRADE

LINER NOTES

ARTIST

LABEL

ALBUM

COUNTRY

CATALOG NO.

YEAR

GRADE

LINER NOTES

ARTIST

LABEL

ALBUM

COUNTRY

CATALOG NO.

YEAR

GRADE

LINER NOTES

ARTIST

LABEL

ALBUM

COUNTRY

CATALOG NO.

YEAR

GRADE

LINER NOTES

ARTIST

LABEL

ALBUM

COUNTRY

CATALOG NO.

YEAR

GRADE

LINER NOTES

ARTIST

LABEL

ALBUM

COUNTRY

CATALOG NO.

YEAR

GRADE

LINER NOTES

ARTIST

LABEL

ALBUM

COUNTRY

CATALOG NO.

YEAR

GRADE

LINER NOTES

ARTIST

LABEL

ALBUM

COUNTRY

CATALOG NO.

YEAR

GRADE

LINER NOTES

ARTIST

LABEL

ALBUM

COUNTRY

CATALOG NO.

YEAR

GRADE

LINER NOTES

ARTIST	LABEL	
ALBUM	COUNTRY	
CATALOG NO.	YEAR	GRADE

LINER NOTES

_____
_____
_____
_____

ARTIST	LABEL	
ALBUM	COUNTRY	
CATALOG NO.	YEAR	GRADE

LINER NOTES

_____
_____
_____
_____

ARTIST	LABEL	
ALBUM	COUNTRY	
CATALOG NO.	YEAR	GRADE

LINER NOTES

_____
_____
_____
_____

ARTIST	LABEL	
ALBUM	COUNTRY	
CATALOG NO.	YEAR	GRADE

LINER NOTES

_____
_____
_____
_____

ARTIST

LABEL

ALBUM

COUNTRY

CATALOG NO.

YEAR

GRADE

LINER NOTES

ARTIST

LABEL

ALBUM

COUNTRY

CATALOG NO.

YEAR

GRADE

LINER NOTES

ARTIST

LABEL

ALBUM

COUNTRY

CATALOG NO.

YEAR

GRADE

LINER NOTES

ARTIST

LABEL

ALBUM

COUNTRY

CATALOG NO.

YEAR

GRADE

LINER NOTES

ARTIST

LABEL

ALBUM

COUNTRY

CATALOG NO.

YEAR

GRADE

LINER NOTES

ARTIST

LABEL

ALBUM

COUNTRY

CATALOG NO.

YEAR

GRADE

LINER NOTES

ARTIST

LABEL

ALBUM

COUNTRY

CATALOG NO.

YEAR

GRADE

LINER NOTES

ARTIST

LABEL

ALBUM

COUNTRY

CATALOG NO.

YEAR

GRADE

LINER NOTES

ARTIST | LABEL
ALBUM | COUNTRY
CATALOG NO. | YEAR | GRADE

LINER NOTES

ARTIST | LABEL
ALBUM | COUNTRY
CATALOG NO. | YEAR | GRADE

LINER NOTES

ARTIST | LABEL
ALBUM | COUNTRY
CATALOG NO. | YEAR | GRADE

LINER NOTES

ARTIST | LABEL
ALBUM | COUNTRY
CATALOG NO. | YEAR | GRADE

LINER NOTES

ARTIST

LABEL

ALBUM

COUNTRY

CATALOG NO.

YEAR

GRADE

LINER NOTES

ARTIST

LABEL

ALBUM

COUNTRY

CATALOG NO.

YEAR

GRADE

LINER NOTES

ARTIST

LABEL

ALBUM

COUNTRY

CATALOG NO.

YEAR

GRADE

LINER NOTES

ARTIST

LABEL

ALBUM

COUNTRY

CATALOG NO.

YEAR

GRADE

LINER NOTES

ARTIST	LABEL	
ALBUM	COUNTRY	
CATALOG NO.	YEAR	GRADE

LINER NOTES

ARTIST	LABEL	
ALBUM	COUNTRY	
CATALOG NO.	YEAR	GRADE

LINER NOTES

ARTIST	LABEL	
ALBUM	COUNTRY	
CATALOG NO.	YEAR	GRADE

LINER NOTES

ARTIST	LABEL	
ALBUM	COUNTRY	
CATALOG NO.	YEAR	GRADE

LINER NOTES

ARTIST

LABEL

ALBUM

COUNTRY

CATALOG NO.

YEAR

GRADE

LINER NOTES

ARTIST

LABEL

ALBUM

COUNTRY

CATALOG NO.

YEAR

GRADE

LINER NOTES

ARTIST

LABEL

ALBUM

COUNTRY

CATALOG NO.

YEAR

GRADE

LINER NOTES

ARTIST

LABEL

ALBUM

COUNTRY

CATALOG NO.

YEAR

GRADE

LINER NOTES

ARTIST

LABEL

ALBUM

COUNTRY

CATALOG NO.

YEAR

GRADE

LINER NOTES

ARTIST

LABEL

ALBUM

COUNTRY

CATALOG NO.

YEAR

GRADE

LINER NOTES

ARTIST

LABEL

ALBUM

COUNTRY

CATALOG NO.

YEAR

GRADE

LINER NOTES

ARTIST

LABEL

ALBUM

COUNTRY

CATALOG NO.

YEAR

GRADE

LINER NOTES

ARTIST | LABEL
ALBUM | COUNTRY
CATALOG NO. | YEAR | GRADE

LINER NOTES

ARTIST | LABEL
ALBUM | COUNTRY
CATALOG NO. | YEAR | GRADE

LINER NOTES

ARTIST | LABEL
ALBUM | COUNTRY
CATALOG NO. | YEAR | GRADE

LINER NOTES

ARTIST | LABEL
ALBUM | COUNTRY
CATALOG NO. | YEAR | GRADE

LINER NOTES

ARTIST

LABEL

ALBUM

COUNTRY

CATALOG NO.

YEAR

GRADE

LINER NOTES

ARTIST

LABEL

ALBUM

COUNTRY

CATALOG NO.

YEAR

GRADE

LINER NOTES

ARTIST

LABEL

ALBUM

COUNTRY

CATALOG NO.

YEAR

GRADE

LINER NOTES

ARTIST

LABEL

ALBUM

COUNTRY

CATALOG NO.

YEAR

GRADE

LINER NOTES

ARTIST

ALBUM

CATALOG NO.

LABEL

COUNTRY

YEAR

GRADE

LINER NOTES

ARTIST

ALBUM

CATALOG NO.

LABEL

COUNTRY

YEAR

GRADE

LINER NOTES

ARTIST

ALBUM

CATALOG NO.

LABEL

COUNTRY

YEAR

GRADE

LINER NOTES

ARTIST

ALBUM

CATALOG NO.

LABEL

COUNTRY

YEAR

GRADE

LINER NOTES

ARTIST

LABEL

ALBUM

COUNTRY

CATALOG NO.

YEAR

GRADE

LINER NOTES

ARTIST

LABEL

ALBUM

COUNTRY

CATALOG NO.

YEAR

GRADE

LINER NOTES

ARTIST

LABEL

ALBUM

COUNTRY

CATALOG NO.

YEAR

GRADE

LINER NOTES

ARTIST

LABEL

ALBUM

COUNTRY

CATALOG NO.

YEAR

GRADE

LINER NOTES

ARTIST | LABEL
ALBUM | COUNTRY
CATALOG NO. | YEAR | GRADE

LINER NOTES

ARTIST | LABEL
ALBUM | COUNTRY
CATALOG NO. | YEAR | GRADE

LINER NOTES

ARTIST | LABEL
ALBUM | COUNTRY
CATALOG NO. | YEAR | GRADE

LINER NOTES

ARTIST | LABEL
ALBUM | COUNTRY
CATALOG NO. | YEAR | GRADE

LINER NOTES

CATEGORY

ARTIST	LABEL	
ALBUM	COUNTRY	
CATALOG NO.	YEAR	GRADE

LINER NOTES

_____

_____

_____

_____

_____

ARTIST	LABEL	
ALBUM	COUNTRY	
CATALOG NO.	YEAR	GRADE

LINER NOTES

_____

_____

_____

_____

_____

ARTIST	LABEL	
ALBUM	COUNTRY	
CATALOG NO.	YEAR	GRADE

LINER NOTES

_____

_____

_____

_____

_____

ARTIST	LABEL	
ALBUM	COUNTRY	
CATALOG NO.	YEAR	GRADE

LINER NOTES

_____

_____

_____

_____

_____

ARTIST

LABEL

ALBUM

COUNTRY

CATALOG NO.

YEAR

GRADE

LINER NOTES

ARTIST

LABEL

ALBUM

COUNTRY

CATALOG NO.

YEAR

GRADE

LINER NOTES

ARTIST

LABEL

ALBUM

COUNTRY

CATALOG NO.

YEAR

GRADE

LINER NOTES

ARTIST

LABEL

ALBUM

COUNTRY

CATALOG NO.

YEAR

GRADE

LINER NOTES

ARTIST	LABEL	
ALBUM	COUNTRY	
CATALOG NO.	YEAR	GRADE

LINER NOTES

ARTIST	LABEL	
ALBUM	COUNTRY	
CATALOG NO.	YEAR	GRADE

LINER NOTES

ARTIST	LABEL	
ALBUM	COUNTRY	
CATALOG NO.	YEAR	GRADE

LINER NOTES

ARTIST	LABEL	
ALBUM	COUNTRY	
CATALOG NO.	YEAR	GRADE

LINER NOTES

ARTIST

LABEL

ALBUM

COUNTRY

CATALOG NO.

YEAR

GRADE

LINER NOTES

ARTIST

LABEL

ALBUM

COUNTRY

CATALOG NO.

YEAR

GRADE

LINER NOTES

ARTIST

LABEL

ALBUM

COUNTRY

CATALOG NO.

YEAR

GRADE

LINER NOTES

ARTIST

LABEL

ALBUM

COUNTRY

CATALOG NO.

YEAR

GRADE

LINER NOTES

ARTIST

LABEL

ALBUM

COUNTRY

CATALOG NO.

YEAR

GRADE

LINER NOTES

ARTIST

LABEL

ALBUM

COUNTRY

CATALOG NO.

YEAR

GRADE

LINER NOTES

ARTIST

LABEL

ALBUM

COUNTRY

CATALOG NO.

YEAR

GRADE

LINER NOTES

ARTIST

LABEL

ALBUM

COUNTRY

CATALOG NO.

YEAR

GRADE

LINER NOTES

ARTIST	LABEL	
ALBUM	COUNTRY	
CATALOG NO.	YEAR	GRADE

LINER NOTES

ARTIST	LABEL	
ALBUM	COUNTRY	
CATALOG NO.	YEAR	GRADE

LINER NOTES

ARTIST	LABEL	
ALBUM	COUNTRY	
CATALOG NO.	YEAR	GRADE

LINER NOTES

ARTIST	LABEL	
ALBUM	COUNTRY	
CATALOG NO.	YEAR	GRADE

LINER NOTES

ARTIST | LABEL

ALBUM | COUNTRY

CATALOG NO. | YEAR | GRADE

LINER NOTES

ARTIST | LABEL

ALBUM | COUNTRY

CATALOG NO. | YEAR | GRADE

LINER NOTES

ARTIST | LABEL

ALBUM | COUNTRY

CATALOG NO. | YEAR | GRADE

LINER NOTES

ARTIST | LABEL

ALBUM | COUNTRY

CATALOG NO. | YEAR | GRADE

LINER NOTES

ARTIST

LABEL

ALBUM

COUNTRY

CATALOG NO.

YEAR

GRADE

LINER NOTES

ARTIST

LABEL

ALBUM

COUNTRY

CATALOG NO.

YEAR

GRADE

LINER NOTES

ARTIST

LABEL

ALBUM

COUNTRY

CATALOG NO.

YEAR

GRADE

LINER NOTES

ARTIST

LABEL

ALBUM

COUNTRY

CATALOG NO.

YEAR

GRADE

LINER NOTES

ARTIST _____ | LABEL _____

ALBUM _____ | COUNTRY _____

CATALOG NO. _____ | YEAR _____ | GRADE _____

LINER NOTES

_____

_____

_____

_____

ARTIST _____ | LABEL _____

ALBUM _____ | COUNTRY _____

CATALOG NO. _____ | YEAR _____ | GRADE _____

LINER NOTES

_____

_____

_____

_____

ARTIST _____ | LABEL _____

ALBUM _____ | COUNTRY _____

CATALOG NO. _____ | YEAR _____ | GRADE _____

LINER NOTES

_____

_____

_____

_____

ARTIST _____ | LABEL _____

ALBUM _____ | COUNTRY _____

CATALOG NO. _____ | YEAR _____ | GRADE _____

LINER NOTES

_____

_____

_____

_____

ARTIST

LABEL

ALBUM

COUNTRY

CATALOG NO.

YEAR

GRADE

LINER NOTES

ARTIST

LABEL

ALBUM

COUNTRY

CATALOG NO.

YEAR

GRADE

LINER NOTES

ARTIST

LABEL

ALBUM

COUNTRY

CATALOG NO.

YEAR

GRADE

LINER NOTES

ARTIST

LABEL

ALBUM

COUNTRY

CATALOG NO.

YEAR

GRADE

LINER NOTES

ARTIST

LABEL

ALBUM

COUNTRY

CATALOG NO.

YEAR

GRADE

LINER NOTES

ARTIST

LABEL

ALBUM

COUNTRY

CATALOG NO.

YEAR

GRADE

LINER NOTES

ARTIST

LABEL

ALBUM

COUNTRY

CATALOG NO.

YEAR

GRADE

LINER NOTES

ARTIST

LABEL

ALBUM

COUNTRY

CATALOG NO.

YEAR

GRADE

LINER NOTES

ARTIST

LABEL

ALBUM

COUNTRY

CATALOG NO.

YEAR

GRADE

LINER NOTES

ARTIST

LABEL

ALBUM

COUNTRY

CATALOG NO.

YEAR

GRADE

LINER NOTES

ARTIST

LABEL

ALBUM

COUNTRY

CATALOG NO.

YEAR

GRADE

LINER NOTES

ARTIST

LABEL

ALBUM

COUNTRY

CATALOG NO.

YEAR

GRADE

LINER NOTES

ARTIST	LABEL	
ALBUM	COUNTRY	
CATALOG NO.	YEAR	GRADE

LINER NOTES

ARTIST	LABEL	
ALBUM	COUNTRY	
CATALOG NO.	YEAR	GRADE

LINER NOTES

ARTIST	LABEL	
ALBUM	COUNTRY	
CATALOG NO.	YEAR	GRADE

LINER NOTES

ARTIST	LABEL	
ALBUM	COUNTRY	
CATALOG NO.	YEAR	GRADE

LINER NOTES

ARTIST

LABEL

ALBUM

COUNTRY

CATALOG NO.

YEAR

GRADE

LINER NOTES

ARTIST

LABEL

ALBUM

COUNTRY

CATALOG NO.

YEAR

GRADE

LINER NOTES

ARTIST

LABEL

ALBUM

COUNTRY

CATALOG NO.

YEAR

GRADE

LINER NOTES

ARTIST

LABEL

ALBUM

COUNTRY

CATALOG NO.

YEAR

GRADE

LINER NOTES

ARTIST	LABEL	
ALBUM	COUNTRY	
CATALOG NO.	YEAR	GRADE

LINER NOTES

_____

_____

_____

_____

ARTIST	LABEL	
ALBUM	COUNTRY	
CATALOG NO.	YEAR	GRADE

LINER NOTES

_____

_____

_____

_____

ARTIST	LABEL	
ALBUM	COUNTRY	
CATALOG NO.	YEAR	GRADE

LINER NOTES

_____

_____

_____

_____

ARTIST	LABEL	
ALBUM	COUNTRY	
CATALOG NO.	YEAR	GRADE

LINER NOTES

_____

_____

_____

_____

ARTIST

LABEL

ALBUM

COUNTRY

CATALOG NO.

YEAR

GRADE

LINER NOTES

ARTIST

LABEL

ALBUM

COUNTRY

CATALOG NO.

YEAR

GRADE

LINER NOTES

ARTIST

LABEL

ALBUM

COUNTRY

CATALOG NO.

YEAR

GRADE

LINER NOTES

ARTIST

LABEL

ALBUM

COUNTRY

CATALOG NO.

YEAR

GRADE

LINER NOTES

ARTIST	LABEL	
ALBUM	COUNTRY	
CATALOG NO.	YEAR	GRADE

LINER NOTES

ARTIST	LABEL	
ALBUM	COUNTRY	
CATALOG NO.	YEAR	GRADE

LINER NOTES

ARTIST	LABEL	
ALBUM	COUNTRY	
CATALOG NO.	YEAR	GRADE

LINER NOTES

ARTIST	LABEL	
ALBUM	COUNTRY	
CATALOG NO.	YEAR	GRADE

LINER NOTES

ARTIST | LABEL

ALBUM | COUNTRY

CATALOG NO. | YEAR | GRADE

LINER NOTES

ARTIST | LABEL

ALBUM | COUNTRY

CATALOG NO. | YEAR | GRADE

LINER NOTES

ARTIST | LABEL

ALBUM | COUNTRY

CATALOG NO. | YEAR | GRADE

LINER NOTES

ARTIST | LABEL

ALBUM | COUNTRY

CATALOG NO. | YEAR | GRADE

LINER NOTES

ARTIST	LABEL	
ALBUM	COUNTRY	
CATALOG NO.	YEAR	GRADE

LINER NOTES

ARTIST	LABEL	
ALBUM	COUNTRY	
CATALOG NO.	YEAR	GRADE

LINER NOTES

ARTIST	LABEL	
ALBUM	COUNTRY	
CATALOG NO.	YEAR	GRADE

LINER NOTES

ARTIST	LABEL	
ALBUM	COUNTRY	
CATALOG NO.	YEAR	GRADE

LINER NOTES

CATEGORY

ARTIST | LABEL
ALBUM | COUNTRY
CATALOG NO. | YEAR | GRADE
LINER NOTES

ARTIST | LABEL
ALBUM | COUNTRY
CATALOG NO. | YEAR | GRADE
LINER NOTES

ARTIST | LABEL
ALBUM | COUNTRY
CATALOG NO. | YEAR | GRADE
LINER NOTES

ARTIST | LABEL
ALBUM | COUNTRY
CATALOG NO. | YEAR | GRADE
LINER NOTES

CATEGORY

ARTIST	LABEL
ALBUM	COUNTRY
CATALOG NO.	YEAR	GRADE

LINER NOTES

ARTIST	LABEL
ALBUM	COUNTRY
CATALOG NO.	YEAR	GRADE

LINER NOTES

ARTIST	LABEL
ALBUM	COUNTRY
CATALOG NO.	YEAR	GRADE

LINER NOTES

ARTIST	LABEL
ALBUM	COUNTRY
CATALOG NO.	YEAR	GRADE

LINER NOTES

ARTIST

LABEL

ALBUM

COUNTRY

CATALOG NO.

YEAR

GRADE

LINER NOTES

ARTIST

LABEL

ALBUM

COUNTRY

CATALOG NO.

YEAR

GRADE

LINER NOTES

ARTIST

LABEL

ALBUM

COUNTRY

CATALOG NO.

YEAR

GRADE

LINER NOTES

ARTIST

LABEL

ALBUM

COUNTRY

CATALOG NO.

YEAR

GRADE

LINER NOTES

ARTIST	LABEL	
ALBUM	COUNTRY	
CATALOG NO.	YEAR	GRADE

LINER NOTES

ARTIST	LABEL	
ALBUM	COUNTRY	
CATALOG NO.	YEAR	GRADE

LINER NOTES

ARTIST	LABEL	
ALBUM	COUNTRY	
CATALOG NO.	YEAR	GRADE

LINER NOTES

ARTIST	LABEL	
ALBUM	COUNTRY	
CATALOG NO.	YEAR	GRADE

LINER NOTES

ARTIST

ALBUM

CATALOG NO.

LABEL

COUNTRY

YEAR

GRADE

LINER NOTES

ARTIST

ALBUM

CATALOG NO.

LABEL

COUNTRY

YEAR

GRADE

LINER NOTES

ARTIST

ALBUM

CATALOG NO.

LABEL

COUNTRY

YEAR

GRADE

LINER NOTES

ARTIST

ALBUM

CATALOG NO.

LABEL

COUNTRY

YEAR

GRADE

LINER NOTES

ARTIST

LABEL

ALBUM

COUNTRY

CATALOG NO.

YEAR

GRADE

LINER NOTES

ARTIST

LABEL

ALBUM

COUNTRY

CATALOG NO.

YEAR

GRADE

LINER NOTES

ARTIST

LABEL

ALBUM

COUNTRY

CATALOG NO.

YEAR

GRADE

LINER NOTES

ARTIST

LABEL

ALBUM

COUNTRY

CATALOG NO.

YEAR

GRADE

LINER NOTES

ARTIST

LABEL

ALBUM

COUNTRY

CATALOG NO.

YEAR

GRADE

LINER NOTES

ARTIST

LABEL

ALBUM

COUNTRY

CATALOG NO.

YEAR

GRADE

LINER NOTES

ARTIST

LABEL

ALBUM

COUNTRY

CATALOG NO.

YEAR

GRADE

LINER NOTES

ARTIST

LABEL

ALBUM

COUNTRY

CATALOG NO.

YEAR

GRADE

LINER NOTES

ARTIST	LABEL	
ALBUM	COUNTRY	
CATALOG NO.	YEAR	GRADE

LINER NOTES

ARTIST	LABEL	
ALBUM	COUNTRY	
CATALOG NO.	YEAR	GRADE

LINER NOTES

ARTIST	LABEL	
ALBUM	COUNTRY	
CATALOG NO.	YEAR	GRADE

LINER NOTES

ARTIST	LABEL	
ALBUM	COUNTRY	
CATALOG NO.	YEAR	GRADE

LINER NOTES

ARTIST | LABEL

ALBUM | COUNTRY

CATALOG NO. | YEAR | GRADE

LINER NOTES

ARTIST | LABEL

ALBUM | COUNTRY

CATALOG NO. | YEAR | GRADE

LINER NOTES

ARTIST | LABEL

ALBUM | COUNTRY

CATALOG NO. | YEAR | GRADE

LINER NOTES

ARTIST | LABEL

ALBUM | COUNTRY

CATALOG NO. | YEAR | GRADE

LINER NOTES

ARTIST	LABEL	
ALBUM	COUNTRY	
CATALOG NO.	YEAR	GRADE

LINER NOTES

ARTIST	LABEL	
ALBUM	COUNTRY	
CATALOG NO.	YEAR	GRADE

LINER NOTES

ARTIST	LABEL	
ALBUM	COUNTRY	
CATALOG NO.	YEAR	GRADE

LINER NOTES

ARTIST	LABEL	
ALBUM	COUNTRY	
CATALOG NO.	YEAR	GRADE

LINER NOTES

ARTIST

ALBUM

CATALOG NO.

LABEL

COUNTRY

YEAR

GRADE

LINER NOTES

ARTIST

ALBUM

CATALOG NO.

LABEL

COUNTRY

YEAR

GRADE

LINER NOTES

ARTIST

ALBUM

CATALOG NO.

LABEL

COUNTRY

YEAR

GRADE

LINER NOTES

ARTIST

ALBUM

CATALOG NO.

LABEL

COUNTRY

YEAR

GRADE

LINER NOTES

CATEGORY

ARTIST

LABEL

ALBUM

COUNTRY

CATALOG NO.

YEAR

GRADE

LINER NOTES

ARTIST

LABEL

ALBUM

COUNTRY

CATALOG NO.

YEAR

GRADE

LINER NOTES

ARTIST

LABEL

ALBUM

COUNTRY

CATALOG NO.

YEAR

GRADE

LINER NOTES

ARTIST

LABEL

ALBUM

COUNTRY

CATALOG NO.

YEAR

GRADE

LINER NOTES

ARTIST	LABEL	
ALBUM	COUNTRY	
CATALOG NO.	YEAR	GRADE

LINER NOTES

ARTIST	LABEL	
ALBUM	COUNTRY	
CATALOG NO.	YEAR	GRADE

LINER NOTES

ARTIST	LABEL	
ALBUM	COUNTRY	
CATALOG NO.	YEAR	GRADE

LINER NOTES

ARTIST	LABEL	
ALBUM	COUNTRY	
CATALOG NO.	YEAR	GRADE

LINER NOTES

ARTIST		LABEL	
ALBUM		COUNTRY	
CATALOG NO.		YEAR	GRADE

LINER NOTES

ARTIST		LABEL	
ALBUM		COUNTRY	
CATALOG NO.		YEAR	GRADE

LINER NOTES

ARTIST		LABEL	
ALBUM		COUNTRY	
CATALOG NO.		YEAR	GRADE

LINER NOTES

ARTIST		LABEL	
ALBUM		COUNTRY	
CATALOG NO.		YEAR	GRADE

LINER NOTES

ARTIST

LABEL

ALBUM

COUNTRY

CATALOG NO.

YEAR

GRADE

LINER NOTES

ARTIST

LABEL

ALBUM

COUNTRY

CATALOG NO.

YEAR

GRADE

LINER NOTES

ARTIST

LABEL

ALBUM

COUNTRY

CATALOG NO.

YEAR

GRADE

LINER NOTES

ARTIST

LABEL

ALBUM

COUNTRY

CATALOG NO.

YEAR

GRADE

LINER NOTES

ARTIST

LABEL

ALBUM

COUNTRY

CATALOG NO.

YEAR

GRADE

LINER NOTES

ARTIST

LABEL

ALBUM

COUNTRY

CATALOG NO.

YEAR

GRADE

LINER NOTES

ARTIST

LABEL

ALBUM

COUNTRY

CATALOG NO.

YEAR

GRADE

LINER NOTES

ARTIST

LABEL

ALBUM

COUNTRY

CATALOG NO.

YEAR

GRADE

LINER NOTES

ARTIST

LABEL

ALBUM

COUNTRY

CATALOG NO.

YEAR

GRADE

LINER NOTES

ARTIST

LABEL

ALBUM

COUNTRY

CATALOG NO.

YEAR

GRADE

LINER NOTES

ARTIST

LABEL

ALBUM

COUNTRY

CATALOG NO.

YEAR

GRADE

LINER NOTES

ARTIST

LABEL

ALBUM

COUNTRY

CATALOG NO.

YEAR

GRADE

LINER NOTES

ARTIST

LABEL

ALBUM

COUNTRY

CATALOG NO.

YEAR

GRADE

LINER NOTES

ARTIST

LABEL

ALBUM

COUNTRY

CATALOG NO.

YEAR

GRADE

LINER NOTES

ARTIST

LABEL

ALBUM

COUNTRY

CATALOG NO.

YEAR

GRADE

LINER NOTES

ARTIST

LABEL

ALBUM

COUNTRY

CATALOG NO.

YEAR

GRADE

LINER NOTES

ARTIST

LABEL

ALBUM

COUNTRY

CATALOG NO.

YEAR

GRADE

LINER NOTES

ARTIST

LABEL

ALBUM

COUNTRY

CATALOG NO.

YEAR

GRADE

LINER NOTES

ARTIST

LABEL

ALBUM

COUNTRY

CATALOG NO.

YEAR

GRADE

LINER NOTES

ARTIST

LABEL

ALBUM

COUNTRY

CATALOG NO.

YEAR

GRADE

LINER NOTES

ARTIST

ALBUM

CATALOG NO.

LINER NOTES

LABEL

COUNTRY

YEAR | GRADE

ARTIST

ALBUM

CATALOG NO.

LINER NOTES

LABEL

COUNTRY

YEAR | GRADE

ARTIST

ALBUM

CATALOG NO.

LINER NOTES

LABEL

COUNTRY

YEAR | GRADE

ARTIST

ALBUM

CATALOG NO.

LINER NOTES

LABEL

COUNTRY

YEAR | GRADE

ARTIST

LABEL

ALBUM

COUNTRY

CATALOG NO.

YEAR

GRADE

LINER NOTES

ARTIST

LABEL

ALBUM

COUNTRY

CATALOG NO.

YEAR

GRADE

LINER NOTES

ARTIST

LABEL

ALBUM

COUNTRY

CATALOG NO.

YEAR

GRADE

LINER NOTES

ARTIST

LABEL

ALBUM

COUNTRY

CATALOG NO.

YEAR

GRADE

LINER NOTES

"I've become more obsessed.
I've never stopped buying vinyl."
—QUESTLOVE

CARE FOR YOUR COLLECTION

To spin an LP and set the needle on its half-mile journey from the outside edge to the center may seem like a simple thing, as it is. But there is power and beauty in that simplicity. To extend the life of your precious vinyl, here are a few things you should know.

REPLACE THE CARTRIDGE EVERY 400 TO 500 HOURS

The tip of the stylus follows the groove at a slow and steady pace, but the contact point between the track and the tip of the stylus is so microscopic that the pounds-per-square-inch add up to somewhere around twenty-six tons (depending on tracking weight). The friction between stylus tip and groove creates temperatures of a few hundred degrees Fahrenheit—even more when the music is loud.

These factoids are fun to marvel at, but they are practical information, too, when contemplating how to care for your fragile collection. It seems like a diamond-tipped stylus would be impervious to the influence of a comparably soft vinyl record, but over the course of a few hundred hours, a stylus will become flat and worn and that diamond tip will morph into a chisel capable of destroying your precious collection, micron by micron. Be gentle with your cartridge and don't forget to replace it.

CLEAN YOUR VINYL WITH EVERY SPIN

There is a common myth that intense heat and pressure generated by the interaction between groove and stylus will melt the vinyl and that we should "cool" our records for a day between spins, but there isn't much evidence to suggest this is actually true. What may damage your records is dust. To fight this fiend, invest immediately in a few inexpensive products:

Carbon-fiber record brush: This tool will control static and remove dust from the surface of your records.

Stylus brush: This smaller brush will help you remove static and dust from your cartridge. Use this and the record brush before and after spinning each side.

Canned air: A record vacuum cleaning machine is the ultimate way to clean a soiled record, but those can set you back a few hundred bucks. Instead, first try canned air to remove dust from deep within the grooves.

When it becomes necessary for a deeper clean, refer to the Library of Congress's website (www.loc.gov/preservation/care/record), which offers a recipe for a reliably safe liquid cleaning solution and instructions on how best to use it. Whatever you do, be cautious not to use any products that may leave a residue.

> Do not touch the grooves. This is where all the precious sonic information is held, and the oil and skin we constantly shed will gunk up the works like superglue in a padlock.

STORE YOUR RECORDS UPRIGHT

Do not stack your records or compact them tightly. The paper sleeves that come with many releases are not optimal for long-term use, as they may scratch or leave pulp in the grooves. It's not a bad idea to have a few dozen high-density polyethylene sleeves on hand with which to swap out your paper ones.

HOW TO VALUE YOUR VINYL

To understand the real value of your vinyl, you need to research the catalog number and grading of each record and reference them against a reputable online or print database. Resources for this include discogs.com, which is like a cross between Wikipedia and eBay for vinyl, or the definitive *Goldmine Record Album Price Guide,* which is the true collector's best friend. Know that an old record does not necessarily mean a valuable one; supply and demand factor greatly in the collectors' marketplace. Remember that a record is only worth what someone will pay for it, so timing can be everything when deciding to sell or buy.

RESEARCH THE CATALOG NUMBER

Locating and researching the catalog numbers of your vinyl records can help you understand what pressing you have, who pressed it, and whether or not it is a bootleg or forgery, and—along with grading the condition of your disc (more on this below)—can help determine the value.

The location of the catalog number varies depending on the company, but look first either on the spine of the cover, in the bar code (often on the back), or on the disc label. It may be a combination of digits and letters. For example, the Beach Boys' 1966 release *Pet Sounds* has the catalog number T2458; Van Halen's *1984* is numbered 1-23985. Different labels use different codes to differentiate their releases, but with a little help from either a handy record album price guide or the employees at your local record store, you can decipher each code to give you all the relevant information you need—and perhaps even some that you don't.

GIVE IT A GRADE

Grading the condition of a vinyl record requires a close inspection of both the disc and the cover. Check each carefully for signs of wear to know what appropriate grade to give the record. If you're buying a record for listening purposes, realize that sometimes a record that sounds great may not look great and a record that looks great may not sound great; if you're deciding whether or not to invest in something that stretches the boundaries of your budget, ask the dealer if you can spin and listen; many shops will have a listening station with headphones and a turntable. If you're buying a vinyl record for collectibility, the look of a disc and its cover will be much more important to you. Scuffs and tears in the cover—even the length of a tear—will determine its grade and its value, so inspect closely.

There are specific definitions of what constitutes a disc's condition; these have been standardized over the years by *Goldmine* magazine's grading system. When grading your vinyl, it's important to be scrupulous—remember that the age of the record will not excuse its condition when it comes to the record's value. Below are brief definitions of each condition; for more information on the subtle differences, turn to goldminemag.com.

Naturally, opposite sides of the two grades will be occupied each by seller and buyer, so it behooves you to understand what constitutes a Very Good Plus (VG+) from Very Good (VG) when negotiating a price. When in doubt, it's always better to underrate a record's condition rather than overpromise.

VINYL GRADES

Mint (M): In flawless condition. Not even as if the record were hermetically sealed fresh off the manufacturing line and buried in a time capsule. More like it somehow jumped through time and space from the moment of production and into your hands. Mint is an extremely rare, practically impossible find in the used-vinyl-records market. Be skeptical of anyone selling anything in "mint condition."

Near Mint/Mint Minus (NM)/(M−): Very nearly mint condition but not quite. Shiny and beautiful with nary even the most subtle of indentations or scuffs on the cover or label. Records in this condition are still rare and highly valuable but, by definition, less valuable than a mint-condition counterpart (should one even exist). This is the highest rating many dealers will ever give.

Very Good Plus/Excellent (VG+)/(E): That nearly Near Mint/Mint Minus copy with one or two very minor visually detectable defects on the cover, label, or disc that do not affect how the disc plays. The disc is still shiny and appears to be Near Mint/Mint Minus at first glance but, alas, is not. Very Good/Good Plus (VG)/(G+): A solid find; particularly valuable to collectors who intend to listen to their vinyl records, as any defects that could have happened naturally through previous careful usage have already happened. It may be neither as shiny nor as beautiful as it once was, but is as excellent a listening experience as it is a value. With proper care, this copy will sound (and look) great for a lifetime.

Very Good (VG): This is a record with scratches that are not just seen but also felt. Or perhaps there are stickers or there is writing on the cover or label. When played, some scratches may be audible, but there are no skips and the louder parts of the recording will cover up most surface noise.

Very Good Minus/Good Plus/Good (VG−)/(G+)/(G): This disc will have lots of surface noise and many tangible scratches but will still play without skipping. The cover art will be noticeably worn around the edges of the disc within and have tears along the edges. If there's a good chance you'll find a copy in better condition, perhaps it's best to hold out.

Fair/Poor (F)/(P): This disc makes a decent, albeit slightly dangerous, Frisbee. Even if it's not cracked, it cannot be played without massive popping and skipping and/or damaging your stylus. If you're looking for an interesting medium for your next art project, this disc may come in handy.

UNDERSTANDING RECORD SPEEDS

There are LPs, 45s, and 78s. Each is unique in the number of revolutions per minute (RPMs) that are required to listen to the recordings and not all turntables have adequate settings for each, so be sure to consider this factor when shopping for a turntable. What follows is some basic information regarding practical facts and key points, but if you're interested in a more intensive look at vinyl's evolution—not only as a consumable product but also as a cultural artifact—check out Dominik Bartmanski and Ian Woodward's book *Vinyl: The Analogue Record in the Digital Age.*

THE LP

When we think of records, what usually come to mind are LPs, or 12-inch "long play" discs. These spin at 33-1/3 RPMs, giving us up to roughly 20 minutes per side. This is how nearly all full-length albums are released today. Fidelity is high, but bear in mind: some colored vinyl is known to not play back as well as black vinyl. That said, there are many releases pressed to colored vinyl that sound (and look) beautiful.

THE 45

This refers to the speed at which the disc is spun. Many of the smaller discs that you will find are referred to as 45s and often have a larger hole in the center. They spin a bit faster, which can mean higher fidelity. Artists will release singles and occasionally EPs in this format, and the limited nature of some of these releases can make them very collectible. You'll need a turntable with a 45-speed setting and a disc-hole adapter to fit the larger hole to the spindle. If you have a turntable that plays only 45s, then you have a really cool thing.

THE 78

Not too common anymore are the 78s, though they have an interesting history and are still occasionally produced. The first flat discs to come after the wax cylinders used at the end of the nineteenth century were spun fast—anywhere from 60 to 130 RPMs—and, in the beginning, were made of very fragile materials. So fragile, in fact, that retailers sold books of empty sleeves designed to hold these discs upright and off the shelf to protect them. Since these books resembled photo albums, releases containing enough music to warrant multiple discs were then referred to as "albums," and the term stuck.

In the early twentieth century, the spin rate of commercial discs began to become standardized to around 78 RPMs, and—since they spun fast and had grooves much wider than on modern LPs—only around four or five minutes of recorded material could fit on a side. Flash forward a few decades: essentially, since pressing technology had improved (which allowed for smaller grooves to fit more closely together) and newer materials were being used (which increased disc durability and reduced surface noise, thus allowing for slower rotation speeds), vinyl record manufacturers ultimately switched to the slower-spinning 33-1/3 RPM LP format to fit more information on a single disc. Still, because of the even higher fidelity possible with faster spinning 78s and the nostalgic value that appeals to many vinyl record collectors, some labels do occasionally release special selections on this format. Get 'em when you can (and make sure you have the appropriate needle to match the wider grooves).

MY MOST-WANTED VINYL

Use these lists to keep track of your favorite artists and memorable albums. You can even tear them out and take them with you to the record store.

ARTIST	ALBUM
YEAR	CATALOG NO.
ARTIST	ALBUM
YEAR	CATALOG NO.
ARTIST	ALBUM
YEAR	CATALOG NO.
ARTIST	ALBUM
YEAR	CATALOG NO.
ARTIST	ALBUM
YEAR	CATALOG NO.
ARTIST	ALBUM
YEAR	CATALOG NO.
ARTIST	ALBUM
YEAR	CATALOG NO.
ARTIST	ALBUM
YEAR	CATALOG NO.
ARTIST	ALBUM
YEAR	CATALOG NO.
ARTIST	ALBUM
YEAR	CATALOG NO.
ARTIST	ALBUM
YEAR	CATALOG NO.

MY MOST-WANTED VINYL

ARTIST	ALBUM
YEAR	CATALOG NO.

ARTIST	ALBUM
YEAR	CATALOG NO.

ARTIST	ALBUM
YEAR	CATALOG NO.

ARTIST	ALBUM
YEAR	CATALOG NO.

ARTIST	ALBUM
YEAR	CATALOG NO.

ARTIST	ALBUM
YEAR	CATALOG NO.

ARTIST	ALBUM
YEAR	CATALOG NO.

ARTIST	ALBUM
YEAR	CATALOG NO.

ARTIST	ALBUM
YEAR	CATALOG NO.

ARTIST	ALBUM
YEAR	CATALOG NO.

ARTIST	ALBUM
YEAR	CATALOG NO.

ARTIST	ALBUM
YEAR	CATALOG NO.

MY MOST-WANTED VINYL

ARTIST	ALBUM
YEAR	CATALOG NO.
ARTIST	ALBUM
YEAR	CATALOG NO.
ARTIST	ALBUM
YEAR	CATALOG NO.
ARTIST	ALBUM
YEAR	CATALOG NO.
ARTIST	ALBUM
YEAR	CATALOG NO.
ARTIST	ALBUM
YEAR	CATALOG NO.
ARTIST	ALBUM
YEAR	CATALOG NO.
ARTIST	ALBUM
YEAR	CATALOG NO.
ARTIST	ALBUM
YEAR	CATALOG NO.
ARTIST	ALBUM
YEAR	CATALOG NO.
ARTIST	ALBUM
YEAR	CATALOG NO.
ARTIST	ALBUM
YEAR	CATALOG NO.

MY MOST-WANTED VINYL

ARTIST	ALBUM
YEAR	CATALOG NO.

ARTIST	ALBUM
YEAR	CATALOG NO.

ARTIST	ALBUM
YEAR	CATALOG NO.

ARTIST	ALBUM
YEAR	CATALOG NO.

ARTIST	ALBUM
YEAR	CATALOG NO.

ARTIST	ALBUM
YEAR	CATALOG NO.

ARTIST	ALBUM
YEAR	CATALOG NO.

ARTIST	ALBUM
YEAR	CATALOG NO.

ARTIST	ALBUM
YEAR	CATALOG NO.

ARTIST	ALBUM
YEAR	CATALOG NO.

ARTIST	ALBUM
YEAR	CATALOG NO.

ARTIST	ALBUM
YEAR	CATALOG NO.

MY MOST-WANTED VINYL

ARTIST	ALBUM
YEAR	CATALOG NO.
ARTIST	ALBUM
YEAR	CATALOG NO.
ARTIST	ALBUM
YEAR	CATALOG NO.
ARTIST	ALBUM
YEAR	CATALOG NO.
ARTIST	ALBUM
YEAR	CATALOG NO.
ARTIST	ALBUM
YEAR	CATALOG NO.
ARTIST	ALBUM
YEAR	CATALOG NO.
ARTIST	ALBUM
YEAR	CATALOG NO.
ARTIST	ALBUM
YEAR	CATALOG NO.
ARTIST	ALBUM
YEAR	CATALOG NO.
ARTIST	ALBUM
YEAR	CATALOG NO.
ARTIST	ALBUM
YEAR	CATALOG NO.

MY MOST-WANTED VINYL

ARTIST	ALBUM
YEAR	CATALOG NO.

ARTIST	ALBUM
YEAR	CATALOG NO.

ARTIST	ALBUM
YEAR	CATALOG NO.

ARTIST	ALBUM
YEAR	CATALOG NO.

ARTIST	ALBUM
YEAR	CATALOG NO.

ARTIST	ALBUM
YEAR	CATALOG NO.

ARTIST	ALBUM
YEAR	CATALOG NO.

ARTIST	ALBUM
YEAR	CATALOG NO.

ARTIST	ALBUM
YEAR	CATALOG NO.

ARTIST	ALBUM
YEAR	CATALOG NO.

ARTIST	ALBUM
YEAR	CATALOG NO.

ARTIST	ALBUM
YEAR	CATALOG NO.

MY MOST-WANTED VINYL

ARTIST	ALBUM
YEAR	CATALOG NO.

ARTIST	ALBUM
YEAR	CATALOG NO.

ARTIST	ALBUM
YEAR	CATALOG NO.

ARTIST	ALBUM
YEAR	CATALOG NO.

ARTIST	ALBUM
YEAR	CATALOG NO.

ARTIST	ALBUM
YEAR	CATALOG NO.

ARTIST	ALBUM
YEAR	CATALOG NO.

ARTIST	ALBUM
YEAR	CATALOG NO.

ARTIST	ALBUM
YEAR	CATALOG NO.

ARTIST	ALBUM
YEAR	CATALOG NO.

ARTIST	ALBUM
YEAR	CATALOG NO.

ARTIST	ALBUM
YEAR	CATALOG NO.

MY MOST-WANTED VINYL

ARTIST	ALBUM
YEAR	CATALOG NO.
ARTIST	ALBUM
YEAR	CATALOG NO.
ARTIST	ALBUM
YEAR	CATALOG NO.
ARTIST	ALBUM
YEAR	CATALOG NO.
ARTIST	ALBUM
YEAR	CATALOG NO.
ARTIST	ALBUM
YEAR	CATALOG NO.
ARTIST	ALBUM
YEAR	CATALOG NO.
ARTIST	ALBUM
YEAR	CATALOG NO.
ARTIST	ALBUM
YEAR	CATALOG NO.
ARTIST	ALBUM
YEAR	CATALOG NO.
ARTIST	ALBUM
YEAR	CATALOG NO.
ARTIST	ALBUM
YEAR	CATALOG NO.

MY MOST-WANTED VINYL

ARTIST	ALBUM
YEAR	CATALOG NO.
ARTIST	ALBUM
YEAR	CATALOG NO.
ARTIST	ALBUM
YEAR	CATALOG NO.
ARTIST	ALBUM
YEAR	CATALOG NO.
ARTIST	ALBUM
YEAR	CATALOG NO.
ARTIST	ALBUM
YEAR	CATALOG NO.
ARTIST	ALBUM
YEAR	CATALOG NO.
ARTIST	ALBUM
YEAR	CATALOG NO.
ARTIST	ALBUM
YEAR	CATALOG NO.
ARTIST	ALBUM
YEAR	CATALOG NO.
ARTIST	ALBUM
YEAR	CATALOG NO.
ARTIST	ALBUM
YEAR	CATALOG NO.

MY MOST-WANTED VINYL

ARTIST	ALBUM
YEAR	CATALOG NO.

ARTIST	ALBUM
YEAR	CATALOG NO.

ARTIST	ALBUM
YEAR	CATALOG NO.

ARTIST	ALBUM
YEAR	CATALOG NO.

ARTIST	ALBUM
YEAR	CATALOG NO.

ARTIST	ALBUM
YEAR	CATALOG NO.

ARTIST	ALBUM
YEAR	CATALOG NO.

ARTIST	ALBUM
YEAR	CATALOG NO.

ARTIST	ALBUM
YEAR	CATALOG NO.

ARTIST	ALBUM
YEAR	CATALOG NO.

ARTIST	ALBUM
YEAR	CATALOG NO.

ARTIST	ALBUM
YEAR	CATALOG NO.

MY MOST-WANTED VINYL

ARTIST	ALBUM
YEAR	CATALOG NO.

ARTIST	ALBUM
YEAR	CATALOG NO.

ARTIST	ALBUM
YEAR	CATALOG NO.

ARTIST	ALBUM
YEAR	CATALOG NO.

ARTIST	ALBUM
YEAR	CATALOG NO.

ARTIST	ALBUM
YEAR	CATALOG NO.

ARTIST	ALBUM
YEAR	CATALOG NO.

ARTIST	ALBUM
YEAR	CATALOG NO.

ARTIST	ALBUM
YEAR	CATALOG NO.

ARTIST	ALBUM
YEAR	CATALOG NO.

ARTIST	ALBUM
YEAR	CATALOG NO.

ARTIST	ALBUM
YEAR	CATALOG NO.

MY MOST-WANTED VINYL

ARTIST	ALBUM
YEAR	CATALOG NO.

ARTIST	ALBUM
YEAR	CATALOG NO.

ARTIST	ALBUM
YEAR	CATALOG NO.

ARTIST	ALBUM
YEAR	CATALOG NO.

ARTIST	ALBUM
YEAR	CATALOG NO.

ARTIST	ALBUM
YEAR	CATALOG NO.

ARTIST	ALBUM
YEAR	CATALOG NO.

ARTIST	ALBUM
YEAR	CATALOG NO.

ARTIST	ALBUM
YEAR	CATALOG NO.

ARTIST	ALBUM
YEAR	CATALOG NO.

ARTIST	ALBUM
YEAR	CATALOG NO.

ARTIST	ALBUM
YEAR	CATALOG NO.

MY MOST-WANTED VINYL

ARTIST	ALBUM
YEAR	CATALOG NO.
ARTIST	ALBUM
YEAR	CATALOG NO.
ARTIST	ALBUM
YEAR	CATALOG NO.
ARTIST	ALBUM
YEAR	CATALOG NO.
ARTIST	ALBUM
YEAR	CATALOG NO.
ARTIST	ALBUM
YEAR	CATALOG NO.
ARTIST	ALBUM
YEAR	CATALOG NO.
ARTIST	ALBUM
YEAR	CATALOG NO.
ARTIST	ALBUM
YEAR	CATALOG NO.
ARTIST	ALBUM
YEAR	CATALOG NO.
ARTIST	ALBUM
YEAR	CATALOG NO.
ARTIST	ALBUM
YEAR	CATALOG NO.

MY MOST-WANTED VINYL

ARTIST	ALBUM
YEAR	CATALOG NO.

ARTIST	ALBUM
YEAR	CATALOG NO.

ARTIST	ALBUM
YEAR	CATALOG NO.

ARTIST	ALBUM
YEAR	CATALOG NO.

ARTIST	ALBUM
YEAR	CATALOG NO.

ARTIST	ALBUM
YEAR	CATALOG NO.

ARTIST	ALBUM
YEAR	CATALOG NO.

ARTIST	ALBUM
YEAR	CATALOG NO.

ARTIST	ALBUM
YEAR	CATALOG NO.

ARTIST	ALBUM
YEAR	CATALOG NO.

ARTIST	ALBUM
YEAR	CATALOG NO.

ARTIST	ALBUM
YEAR	CATALOG NO.